The Art of Poetry volume 2

Forward: *Poems of the Decade anthology*

Published by Peripeteia Press Ltd.

First published January 2016

ISBN: 978-0-9930778-7-6

Peripeteia.webs.com

Contents

General Introduction to the The Art of Poetry series

The philosopher Nietzsche described his work as 'the greatest gift that (mankind) has ever been given'. The Elizabethan poet Edmund Spencer hoped his book **The Faerie Queene** would transform its readers into noblemen. In comparison, our aims for *The Art of Poetry* series of books are a little more modest. Fundamentally we aim to provide books that will be of maximum use to English students and their teachers. In our experience few students before A-level, and not all students at this level, read essays on poetry, yet, whatever specification they are studying, they have to write analytical essays on poetry. So, we've offering some models, written in a lively and accessible style. In Volume 1 we chose canonical poems for a number of reasons: Firstly they are simply great poems, well worth reading and studying; secondly we chose poems from across time so that they sketch in outline major developments in English poetry, from the Elizabethan period up until the present day. And, being canonical poems, they often crop up on GCSE and A-level specifications, so our material will be useful critical accompaniment and revision material.

This current book, volume 2 is, however, dedicated to modern poetry, in particular, to the **Forward Poems of the Decade** anthology. Hence, taken as a whole, **The Art of Poetry** series will cover a rich and varied range of literature, from poems that have endured years of critical readings to ones on which very little has been written, until now that is.

Introduction to *volume 2: Poems of the Decade*

Squeezed into dingy corners of bookshops, squeezed almost entirely out of newspapers, squeezed thin to the point of invisibility in the media (with the honourable exception of radio 4) modern poets desperately need the oxygen of this rare exposure to a young, vibrant audience. Forward's *Poems of the Decade* anthology features a great, rich range of voices, styles, forms and views, and in its pages the reader discovers many of the most outstanding poetic voices of this generation, writing about the world around us now.

Edexcel examination board made a bold and commendable decision to make a modern poetry anthology a set text for both their new AS and A-level English Literature specifications. It's rare to see such an innovative text choice and we think there's something refreshing and invigorating about encountering literature that has not already been endlessly critiqued, discussed and argued over by academics and critics. These poems are not weighed down by critical baggage and neither therefore is the reader. Sometimes secondary sources can obscure our perceptions of the original texts. Reading a canonical poem students join the back of a very long queue of other readers. Reading and writing about Forward's anthology gives students and teachers the chance to stand right at the front and, with their own responses, to take part in shaping the emerging critical landscape around this anthology.

Being the first critics will be exciting, but it's also a challenging task. Performing the tight-rope walk of interpretation without the safety net of other readers can be daunting and make us feel exposed, uncertain of our bearings. In an examination situation, where the stakes are so high, the task might feel even more intimidating. We think some support might be welcome. The essays in this volume of *The Art of Poetry* are not intended to replace students' own reading of the poems; the fundamental job of an A-level English reader is to grapple with the set texts themselves and to construct their own readings from this direct interaction with the source material. Nor are these essays designed to provide model answers to be remembered and repeated in examination conditions. Rather they are meant as springboards; we hope they will stimulate discussion, that you will find things you agree with but also things with which you disagree. And, in both cases, interacting with our readings should help consolidate your own. So, these essays are sounding boards too against which you can test your own ideas. We'd like to say our essays are body boards too, because they're fun to ride/read and will carry you with their own momentum. But obviously that's an analogy that just takes things a bit too far. Overall, our hope is that reading these essays will lead you back into re-reading the poems themselves with greater avidity.

Our primary audience for this book is A-level students, but we've included teaching ideas that we hope might be of use to colleagues. (We've used the utterly unoriginal, but universally understood sign of the light bulb to signify a teaching idea. At the back of the book there's also a list of tried and tested revision activities which can be completed individually or with a class.) It's a brave step for English teachers to choose this anthology; there are no 'how to teach' guides or (currently) York Notes or such like, for this text; the onus is on the expertise and creativity of teachers to make this text work in a classroom. Fortunately, though I say it myself as a practising English teacher, English teachers enjoy this sort of creative challenge and are usually very good at them. A little support will, we hope, be useful.

Edexcel's exam questions require comparison of poems both at AS and A-level. At AS students will have a choice of two questions, each of which will ask them to compare a poem of their choice with one chosen by the Edexcel examiners. Unsurprisingly, at A-level the task is a little stiffer. Here a poem from the Forward anthology will have to be compared with an 'unseen' poem. As teachers, we are well aware of the demands of writing about 'unseen' material, so in the next section of this introduction we offer some advice about how to tackle the unseen. We'll also say a few things about comparing texts.

Modern British poetry

To misquote Andrew Marvell a little, had we but space enough and time we would, of course, provide a comprehensive overview of developments in British poetry from Thomas Hardy through to the most recently published work. Unfortunately, or perhaps, fortunately for you, we do not have the space or time to produce this here. And, to be honest, nor do A-level students or their teachers need a comprehensive literary context for *Poems of the Decade*. Marks in the Edexcel exam, will be rewarded for quality of reading and writing and for the strength of the comparison. There are no marks for context. Hence we have not written short potted biographies for each poet in the following essays. In any case, a little research on the internet will provide this information for the diligent student. If you are curious enough to want a comprehensive treatment, we strongly recommend *The Oxford English Literary History, volume 12, Part II*, by Randall Stevenson.

If there are no marks for context, why read this? Because context is always enriching. An understanding of the literary context deepens appreciation of any text. Context may not determine meanings, but it certainly has a significant effect. Consider, for instance, the following sentence, 'the duck is ready to eat'. How does the meaning of this sentence change if we change the context? If the context is a restaurant one meaning is clear. But a different meaning is evinced if the context is a pond. So, whether they are officially rewarded through assessment objectives or not, contexts (literary, socio-historical and of reception) are always significant.

Mainstream and the avant-garde

In all forms of art there is a mainstream and an avant-garde. After T. S. Eliot launched **The Waste Land** on an unsuspecting public in the 1920s and the Modernist Movement swept through the arts world a split opened up in English poetry that still, arguably, persists to this day. On one side were poets committed to the sort of radical thematic, stylistic and formal experimentalism that Modernism promoted. On the other were poets who wanted to ignore

Modernism and maintain the continuity with earlier, traditional English poetry.

Modernist texts are characterised by a collage approach. Incongruous elements are combined, so that structurally and linguistically they are often an assembly of fragments. Generally interested in the mind and the workings of the subconscious, such texts explore topics traditionally oulawed as taboo. For example, in novels, Modernists develop the 'stream of consciousness' to reveal subconscious drives governing characters' behaviour. Often drawing on classical literature as a form of ironic intertextual contrast, Modernist works also tend to be self-reflexive - in dialogue with themselves and their own procedures. As anyone who has read *The Waste Land* or tried to read Joyce's seminal Modernist novel, *Ulysses,* will know, Modernist texts tend to be hard to understand and their subject matter challenging. Consider, for instance, Picasso's famous painting *Les Demoiselles d'Avignon*, first exhibited in 1907, and a prime example of early Modernism in the visual arts:

Not exactly a conventional depiction of the female nude is it?

In contrast, traditionalist poets eschewed what they considered to be the self-indulgent excesses, elitism and brain-bending difficulties of Modernism, valuing instead well-crafted, sonorous and coherent poems which aimed to communicate comprehensible meaning to a wider audience. Focusing on capturing 'the real', antipathetic to anything smacking of redundant Romanticism, illogical mysticism or foreign fancy avant-gardism, these poets championed traditional craft skills of writing, embodied for them in the work of the Victorian poet, Thomas Hardy, pictured here. In the 1950s and 60s a group of poets developed who gave the emphasis on well-made poems a contemporary, down-to-earth, restrained, peculiarly English spin. Known as **The Movement** poets, they developed a poetic aesthetic that dominated the mainstream of English poetry for many decades. Arguably, indeed, their ideas still have a powerful influence on contemporary poetry.

Movement poets often took an ironic observatory role to comment on the vagaries of modern culture. Often they combined traditional, regular poetic forms with modern, colloquial English and arch references to popular culture. Philip Larkin is the most famous poet associated with The Movement. Though other strains kicked against this mainstream, notably the work of Ted Hughes and Sylvia Plath and, in America, the rhapsodic style of the Beat poets, Movement aesthetic, as we have said, persisted into the late twentieth century as the dominant one in English poetry.

The approach of the other side of the divide was well articulated by Iain Sinclair in the provocative introduction to his radical anthology of English poetry, which, even in its title sticks a metaphorical two fingers up to The

Movement and its followers. Sinclair's anthology **Conductors of Chaos** was first published in 1996. Here's a taste of the introduction:

> The work I value is that which seems most remote, alienated, fractured. I don't claim to 'understand' it but I like having it around. The darker it grows outside the window, the worse the noises from the island, the more closely do I attend to the mass of instant-printed pamphlets that pile up around my desk. The very titles are pure adrenalin: *Satyrs and Mephitic Angels, Tense Fodder, Hellhound Memos, Civic Crime, Alien Skies, Harpmest Intermezzi, A Pocket History of the Soul.* You don't need to read them, just handle them: feel the sticky heat creep up through your fingers....Why should they be easy? Why should they not reflect some measure of the complexity of the climate in which they exist? Why should we not be prepared to make an effort, to break sweat, in hope of high return?

Sinclair goes on to offer some interesting advice on how to read any poem, but especially a radical, avant-garde one:

> There's no key, no Masonic password: take the sequence gently, a line at a time. Treat the page as a block, sound it for submerged sonar effects. Suspend conditioned reflexes...if it comes too sweetly, somebody is trying to sell you something.

Try placing all the set poems in the Forward Anthology on a continuum from, at one end, avant-garde/ radical/ experimental and at the other end mainstream/ traditional/ well-made. Repeat the exercise, only this time arrange the poems by their various constituent elements, form, language, themes. Some poems, might, for instance, be radical in terms of content, but more conventional in form, or vice versa. At the end of this process you should develop a sense of which poem is the most radical and which the most traditional in approach. Which is better, or, indeed, whether one style is better than another, is for you to judge.

Tackling the unseen

If Literature is a jungle, of all the beasts that roam or lurk among its foliage, from the enormous, lumbering Victorian state-of-the-nation novel to the carnivorous revenge tragedy, the most dangerous by far is a small, fast-moving beast, a beast un-tethered by place or time, a beast that is, in fact invisible. This infamous critter is called, simply, 'the unseen'.

Well, that's sounds all rather alarming. Let's bring the rhetoric down a notch or ten. How should you go about analysing an unseen poem and how can you prepare for this demanding task?

To start with, we don't believe that there's one universally right method for reading poems. If there were, all the varied types of literary theorists - Feminist, Marxist, poststructuralist, postcolonial and so forth – would have to adopt the same working methods. Like the children depicted below, critics and

theorists do not, in fact, all read in the same way. So, it's vital to appreciate that there's no single master key that will unlock all poems. A uniformly applicable method of reading a poem, or of writing about it in an examination, or for coursework, is like the philosopher's stone; it just does not exist. Or as Iain Sinclair puts it, there's no 'Masonic password' that will give you instant access to the inner chamber of a poem's secret meanings.

Having a singular method also makes the foolish assumption that all poems can be analysed in exactly the same way. A mathematician who thinks all maths problems can be solved with one method probably won't get very far, we expect. Instead you need to be flexible and trust your own trained reading skills. Respond to the key features of the text that is in front of you as you see them. It's no good thinking you will always write your second paragraph on figurative imagery, for instance, because what are you going to do when confronted with a poem entirely devoid of this feature? Although all the essays in this book explore key aspects of poetry, such as language, form, themes, effects and so forth, we haven't approached these aspects in a rigid, uniform or mechanical way. Rather our essays are shaped by what we found most engaging about each poem. For some poems this may be the use the poet has made of form; for others it might be imagery; for others still it might be the way the poet orchestrates language to bring out its musical properties. In terms of critical approach, we'd champion well-informed freedom above over-regulated and imposed conformity. Hence, we hope our essays will be varied and interesting and a little bit unpredictable, a bit like the poems themselves. We trust that if you write about how a poet's techniques contribute to the exploration of themes and generation of effect you won't be going far wrong. (If you're interested in trying different methods of analysing poems, there is a concise guide in our A-level companion book, *The Art of Writing English Literature essays, for A-level and Beyond*).

So to reiterate: Always keep to the fore of your essay the significance and impact of the material you're analysing. Very sophisticated analysis involves exploring how different aspects of the poem work in consort to generate effects. As a painter uses shapes, brush strokes, colours and so forth, or a composer uses chords, notes and time signatures, so a poet has a range of poetic devices at his or her disposal.

Think of a poem as a machine built to remember itself. Your task is to take apart the poem's precision engineering - the various cogs, gears and wheels that make the poem go - and to examine carefully how they work. If you can also explain how they combine together to generate the poem's ideas and feelings you will, without a shadow of a doubt, achieve top marks.

We believe your essays must express your own thoughts and feelings, informed by the discipline of literary study and by discussion with your teachers and peers. And, that your essays should be expressed in your own emerging critical voice. Finding, refining and then trusting your critical voice is part of the self-discovery that contributes to making English Literature such a rewarding subject to study at A-level.

Offering quality support material, a safety net, if you like, for your walk on the tightrope of interpretation, we hope to give you confidence to make it across to the other side. And in achieving this, to also achieve great grades in your exams.

Writing comparative essays

The following is adapted from our discussion of this topic in *The Art of Writing English Literature Essays* course companion book, and is a briefer, nuts and bolts version, tailored to the Edexcel exam task. Fundamentally comparative essays want you to display not only your ability to intelligently talk about literary texts, but also your ability to make meaningful connections between them. The first starting point is your topic. This must be broad enough to allow substantial thematic overlapping of the texts. However, too little overlap and it will be difficult to connect the texts; too much overlap and your discussion will be lopsided and one-dimensional. In the case of the Edexcel exam, the board will determine the topic they want you to discuss. The exam question will ask you to focus on the methods used by the poets to explore a particular theme. You will also be directed to write specifically on themes, language and imagery as well as other poetic techniques.

One poem from the set text will be specified. You will then have to choose a companion poem. Selecting the right poem for interesting comparison is obviously very important. To think about this visually, you don't want Option A, below, [not enough overlap] or Option B [two much overlap]. You want Option C. This option allows substantial common links to be built between your chosen texts where discussion arises from both fundamental similarities AND differences.

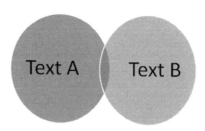

Option A: too many differences

Option B: too many similarities

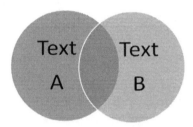

Option C: suitable number of similarities and differences

The final option will generate the most interesting discussion as it will allow substantial similarities to emerge as well as differences. <u>The best comparative essays actually find that what seemed like clear similarities become subtle differences and vice versa</u> while still managing to find rock solid similarities to build their foundations on.

How should you structure your comparative essay? Consider the following structures. Which one is best and why?

Essay Structure #1
1. Introduction
2. Main body paragraph #1 - Text A
3. Main body paragraph #2 - Text A
4. Main body paragraph #3 - Text B
5. Main body paragraph #4 - Text B
6. Conclusion

Essay Structure #2

1. Introduction
2. Main body paragraph #1 - Text A
3. Main body paragraph #2 - Text A
4. Main body paragraph #3 - Text B
5. Main body paragraph #4 - Text B
6. Comparison of main body paragraphs #1 & #3 - Text A + B
7. Comparison of main body paragraphs #2 & #4 - Text A + B
8. Conclusion

Essay Structure #3

1. Introduction
2. Main body paragraph #1 - Text A + B
3. Main body paragraph #2 - Text A + B
4. Main body paragraph #3 - Text A + B
5. Main body paragraph #4 - Text A+ B
6. Conclusion

We hope you will agree that 3 is the optimum option. Option 1 is the dreaded 'here is everything I know about text A, followed by everything I know by Text B' approach where the examiner has to work out what the connections are between the texts. This will score the lowest AO4 marks. Option 2 is better: There is some attempt to compare the two texts. However, it is a very inefficient way of comparing the two texts. For comparative essay writing the most important thing is to discuss both texts together. This is the most effective and efficient way of achieving your overall aim. Option 3 does this by comparing and contrasting the two texts under common umbrella headings. This naturally encourages comparison. Using comparative discourse markers, such as 'similarly', 'in contrast to', 'conversely' 'likewise' and 'however' also facilitates effective comparison.

When writing about each poem keep the bullet points in mind. Make sure you do not work chronologically through a poem, summarising the content of each stanza. Responses of this sort typically start with 'In the first stanza' and employ discourse markers of time rather than comparison, such as 'after', 'next', 'then' and so forth. Even if your reading is analytical rather than summative your essay should not work through the poem from the opening to the ending. Instead, make sure you write about the ideas explored in both texts (themes), the feelings and effects generated and the techniques the poet's employ to achieve these.

Writing about language

Poems are paintings as well as windows: We look at them as well as through them. As you know, we have to pay special attention to language in poetry because of all the literary art forms poetry, in particular, employs language in a self-conscious and distinctive way. We can break down the analysis of language into a number of different categories:

- By **diction** we mean the vocabulary used in a poem. A poem might be composed from the ordinary language of everyday speech or it might use elaborate, technical or elevated phrasing. Or both.
- **Grammatically** a poem may use complex sentences, or employ a lot of adjectives. Or it may rely extensively on nouns and verbs connected in simple sentences. Picking out and exploring words from specific grammatical classes has the merit of being incisive and usually illuminating.
- Poets might mix together different types, conventions and registers of language, moving, for example, between formal and informal, spoken and written, and so forth. Arranging the diction in the poem in terms of **lexico-semantic fields**, by register or by etymology, helps reveal these underlying patterns of meaning.
- For almost all poems **imagery** is a crucial aspect of language. Broadly imagery is a synonym for description and can be broken down into two types, **sensory and figurative**. Figurative imagery, in particular, is always significant. Not all poems rely on metaphors and similes; these devices are only part of a poet's repertoire, but figurative language is always important when it occurs because it compresses multiple meanings into itself. To use a technical term figurative images are polysemic, they contain many meanings. Try writing out the all the meanings contained in a metaphor in a more concise and economical way. Even simple, everyday metaphors compress meaning in this way. If we want to say our teacher is fierce and powerful and that we fear his or her wrath we can more concisely say our teacher is a monster.

Writing about patterns of sound

What not to do: Tempting as it may be to spot sonic features of a poem and list these, don't do this. Avoid something along the lines of "The poet uses alliteration here and the rhyme scheme is ABABCDCDEFEFGG." Sometimes, indeed, it may be tempting to set out the poem's whole rhyme scheme like this. Resist the temptation: This sort of identification of features is worth zero marks. Marks in exams are reserved for attempts to link techniques to meanings and to effects.

Probably many of us have been sitting in English lessons listening somewhat sceptically as our English teacher explains the surprisingly specific significance of some seemingly random piece of alliteration in a poem. Something along the lines "The double d sounds here reinforce a sense of invincible strength" or "the harsh repetition of the 't' sounds suggests anger". Through all of our minds at some point may have passed the idea that, in these instances, English teachers appear to be using some sort of Enigma-style secret symbolic decoding machine that reveals how particular patterns of sounds have such particular coded meanings.

And this sort of thing is not all nonsense. Originally deriving from an oral tradition, poems are, of course, written for the ear as much as for the eye, to be heard as much as read. A poem is a soundscape as much as it is a set of meanings. Sounds are, however, difficult to tie to very definite meanings and effects. By way of example, the old BBC radiophonic workshop, which produced ambient sounds for radio and television programmes, used the same sounds in different contexts, knowing that the audience would perceive them in the appropriate way because of that context. Hence the sound of bacon sizzling, of an audience clapping and of feet walking over gravel were actually recordings of an identical sound. Listeners heard them differently because of the context. So, we may, indeed, be able to spot the repeated 's' sounds in a poem, but whether this creates a hissing sound like a snake or the susurration of the sea will depend on the context within the poem and the ears of the reader. Whether a sound is soft and soothing or harsh and grating is also open to interpretation.

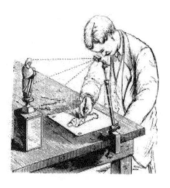

The idea of connecting these sounds to meanings or significance is also a good one. Your analysis will be most convincing if you use a number of pieces of evidence together. In other words, rather than try to pick out individual examples of sonic effects we recommend you explore the weave or pattern of sounds, the effects these generate and their contribution to feelings and ideas. For example, this might mean examining how alliteration and assonance are used together to achieve a particular mimetic effect. An example will help demonstrate what we mean.

In John Burnside's poem, **History,** he describes bits and bobs of debris found on a beach in the following way:

Sna**il shells, shr**e**ds** of r**a**zorfish;
Smu**dge**s of w**ee**d and fl**e**sh** on tideworn **st**one

Sonically, fragile detritus is made to appear solid and significant. Sibilance connects many of the words together. The cohesive sonic effect this generates is reinforced by the weave of other sounds:

- soft 'sh' sounds
- alliteration of 'w'
- assonance of 'a' s and of 'e's, the latter lengthen to 'ee' in 'weed'
- consonantal half rhyme of 'fish' and 'flesh'.
- a 'dge' rhyme sound carried from 'shreds' to 'smudge'

In concert, a rich, musical soundworld is constructed. The effect here is clear; to appreciate the full significance you'll need to read the essay on this poem.

Writing about form & structure

As you know by now, there are no marks for simply identifying textual features. This holds true for language, sounds and for form. Consider the relationship between a poem's form and its themes and effects. Broadly speaking the form can either work with or against a poem's content. Conventionally a sonnet, for instance, is about love, whereas a limerick is a comic form. A serious love poem in the form of a limerick would be unusual.

Start off taking a panoramic perspective: Think of the forest, not the trees. Don't even read the words, just look at the poem on the page, like a painting. Is the poem slight, thin, fat, long, short? What is the relation of whiteness to blackness? A poem about a long winding river will probably look rather different from one about a small pebble. Think, for instance, about how Eavan Boland uses form in *Inheritance* to convey a sense of contemplative thought. How does the visual layout of the poem relate to what it is about? Does this form enhance or create a tension against the content? Is the form one you can recognise, like a sonnet?

Zoom in: Explore the stanza form, lineation, enjambement and caesura. Focus in on specific examples and on points of transition. For instance, if a poem has four regular quatrains followed by a couplet examine the effect of this change. Consider regularity. Closed forms of poems, such as sonnets, are highly regular with set rhyme schemes, metre and number of lines. The opposite form is called 'open', the most extreme version of which is free verse. In free verse poems the poet dispenses with any set metre, rhyme scheme or recognisable traditional form. Try placing the poems from the Forward anthology on a continuum from regular to irregular, from closed to free verse.

Nice to metre...

A brief guide to metre and rhythm in poetry

Why express yourself in poetry? Why read words dressed up and expressed as a poem? What do can you get from poetry that can't from prose? There are many compelling answers to these questions. Here, though, we're going to concentrate on one aspect of the unique appeal of poetry – the structure of sound in poetry. Whatever our stage of education, we are all already sophisticated at detecting and using structured sound. Try reading the following sentences without any variation whatsoever in how each sound is  emphasised, and they will quickly lose what essential human characteristics they have. The sentences will sound robotic. So, in a sense, we won't be teaching anything new here. It's just that in poetry the structure of sound is carefully unusually crafted and created. It becomes a key part of what a poem is.

We will introduce a few new key technical terms along the way, but the ideas are straightforward. Individual sounds (syllables) are either stressed (emphasised, sounding louder and longer) or unstressed. As well as clustering into words and sentences for meaning, these sounds (syllables) cluster into rhythmic groups or feet, producing the poem's metre, which is the characteristic way its rhythm works.

In some poems the rhythm is very regular and may even have a name, such as iambic pentameter. At the other extreme a poem may have no discernible regularity at all. As we have said, this is called free verse. It is vital to remember that the sound in a good poem is structured so that it combines effectively with the meanings.

For example, take a look at these two lines from Marvell's *To his Coy Mistress*:

'But at my back I alwaies hear
Times winged Chariot hurrying near:'

Forgetting the rhythms for a moment, Marvell is basically saying at this point 'Life is short, Time flies, and it's after us'. Now concentrate on the rhythm of his words.

- In the first line every other syllable is stressed: 'at', 'back', 'al', 'hear'.
- Each syllable before these is unstressed 'But', 'my', 'I', 'aies'.
- This is a regular beat or rhythm which we could write
  ti TUM / ti TUM / ti TUM / ti TUM , with the / separating the feet. ('Feet' is the technical term for metrical units of sound)
- This type of two beat metrical pattern is called **iambic**, and because there are four feet in the line, it is **tetrameter**. So this line is in 'iambic tetrameter'. (Tetra is Greek for four)
- Notice that 'my' and 'I' being unstressed diminishes the speaker, and we are already prepared for what is at his 'back', what he can 'hear' to be bigger than him, since these sounds are stressed.
- On the next line, the iambic rhythm is immediately broken off, since the next line hits us with two consecutive stressed syllables straight off: 'Times' 'wing'. Because a pattern had been established, when it suddenly changes the reader feels it, the words feel crammed together more urgently, the beats of the rhythm are closer, some little parcels of time have gone missing.

A physical rhythmic sensation is created of time slipping away, running out. This subtle sensation is enhanced by the stress-unstress-unstress pattern of words that follow, 'chariot hurrying' (TUM-ti-ti, TUM-ti-ti). So the hurrying sounds underscore the meaning of the words.

13 ways of looking at a poem

1. <u>Crunch it (1)</u> – This means re-ordering all of the text in the poem under grammatical headings of nouns, verbs, prepositions and so forth. If this is done before reading the poem for the first time, the students' task is (a) to try to create a poem from this material and (b) to work out what they can about the style and themes of the original poem from these dislocated grammatical aspects. An alternative is to list the words alphabetically and do same exercise. You'll see we suggest something along these lines for Simon Armitage's poem. Re-arranging the poem in grammatical categories after reading can also be a useful analytical task.

2. <u>Crunch it (2)</u> – This is another exercise that can be used as an introductory activity before reading a poem for the first time or as a useful revision task. Rearrange the poem into groupings based on lexico-semantic fields. Show students one group of words at a time, asking them to write down what the each group of words might tell us about the poem's themes & style. Alternatively, split the class into small groups and give each one group of words. Ask them to suggest possible titles for the poem.

3. <u>Crunch it (3)</u> – In this method students have to reduce each line of the poem to one key word. If they do this individually, then in pairs, then as a class, it can facilitate illuminating whole class discussion and bring out different readings. We've applied the cruncher at the end of each of the following essays.

4. <u>Cloze it</u> (aka blanket-blank) – A cloze exercise helps students to focus on specific choices of vocabulary. Blank out a few important words in the first couple of stanzas and as much as you dare of the rest of the

poem. Make this task harder as the course goes on. Or use it for revision to see how well the poem's been remembered.

5. Shuffle it – Give students all the lines in the poem but in the wrong order. Their task is to find the right order. Make this a physical exercise; even older pupils like sticking cut up pieces of paper together! Start off with reasonably easy activities. Then make them fiendishly hard.

6. Split it – Before a first reading, post a few key lines from the poem around the classroom, like clues for literary detectives. Arrange the class into small groups. Each group analyses only a few lines. Feedback to the class what they have found out, what they can determine about the poem. Ask them how the information from other groups confirms/ changes their thoughts. Finish by getting them to sequence the lines.

7. Transform it – Turn the poem into something else, a storyboard for a film version, a piece of music or drama, a still image, a collage of images a piece of performance art. Engage your and their creativity.

8. Switch it – Swap any reference to gender in the poem and the gender of the poet. Change every verb or noun or metaphor or smile in the poem. Compare with the non-doctored version; what's revealed?

9. Pastiche or parody it – Ask students to write a poem in the style of one of the poems from the anthology. Take printed copies in. Add your own and one other poem. See if the students can recognise the published poem from the imitations. A points system can add to the fun.

10. Match it (1) – Ask students to find an analogue for the poem. Encourage them to think metaphorically. If they think Burnside's *History* is like a thrash metal song by the *The Frenzied Parsnips* they'll really need to explain how.

11. <u>Match it (2)</u> – Take some critical material on about 5 or 6 poets; there's good stuff on the **Poetry by Heart** and Poetry Archive websites. Take one poem by each of these poets and a photo. Mix this material up on one page of A3. The students' task is to match the poet to the critical material and to the image. To add to the creative fun you could make up a poem, poet and critical comments.

12. <u>Complete it</u> - Give the students the first few lines of the poem. Their task is to complete it. If they get stuck and plead profusely and if you're feeling especially generous you can give them a few clues, such as the rhyme scheme or the stanza form.

13. <u>Write back to</u> . If the poem's a dramatic monologue, like Patience Agbabi's *Eat Me* change the point of view and write the man's version of events. What might be the silent hunter's thoughts in Vicki Feaver's *The Gun*? What might the young woman have to say if she could reply to Sue Boyle's poem *A Leisure Centre is also a Temple of Learning*?

14. <u>Listen to it</u> - Tell the class you're going to read the poem once. Their task is to listen carefully and then write down as much of it as they can remember, working first on their own and then in pairs. Read the poem a second time and repeat the exercise. Discuss what they did and didn't remember.

Yes, we know that's 14 things to do with a poem. Think of the last one as a bonus.

Forward Poems of the Decade

Poetry is when an emotion has found its thought and the thought has found words.

Robert Frost

David Herd: *the importance of the title*

The shortest poem in the anthology is not on the Edexcel set list. But it makes for a good lesson starter activity on the significance of titles.

The poem is by academic & poet David Herd and is just two lines long:

Worked in the morning.
Watched TV.

What can we say about such a short, seemingly inconsequential poem? How could it possibly have been selected from all the other hundreds of poems for *Forward Poems of the Decade*? Is this, perhaps, another example of the sort of craziness that often gives modern art such a bad name? Is it, maybe, some sort of game about how we construct a poem by reading it as such? Could it just as easily have been:

Maybe some sort of game.
About how we construct
A poem by reading it as such.

Let's suppress our inner Daily Mail-appalled-common-sense reader for a moment and give the poet and the anthologisers the benefit of the doubt, for now, at least and treat the two lines of the poem to the same level of analysis as would to any literary masterwork. Clearly the poem is composed of very ordinary, everyday language and outlines a very ordinary, seemingly insignificant experience. Probably most of us do this or something like this each day and few of us would think of writing a poem about something so utterly mundane. And if we did, we'd probably be tempted to try and jazz it up a bit. But, there are none of the usual poetic techniques, such as imagery or sonic effects, here. Both of the two sentences are incomplete fragments, denuded of a subject, which we take to be 'I'. This helps create the impression of someone speaking, perhaps. They are blunt, truncated and seemingly plain statements of fact - technically both sentences are declaratives. Plainess of language matches the ordinary experience. But so what? We could say the same for the language on a bus ticket.

So, let's keep at it: Each of the two lines ends with an emphatic full stop, so that the two experiences of work and leisure seem disconnected. Maybe there's the suggestion that only these two things mattered for some reason. Why, for instance, aren't there further lines outlining other quotidian experiences, such as 'drank some tea', 'drove home', 'cooked the dinner'? So, something about watching the TV at this point must have been very important.

After spending as long as you or your class can stomach on analysing the poem's six words, the next task is to suggest possible titles for the poem. Here are a few my cynical year 11 class suggested: *Life, School, What I learnt today, The shortest poem with the longest possible title we could think of.* Once the class have tired of this you can reveal the poem's actual title: **September 11th, 2001**. Now discuss what difference the title makes.

Patience Agbabi: *eat me*

In terms of form, Agbabi's poem is a dramatic monologue written in the voice of an obese woman kept in some sort of captivity by a perverse male lover. According to **The Oxford Companion of English Literature** a dramatic monologue is a poem 'delivered as though by a single imagined person, frequently but not always to an imagined auditor: the speaker is not to be identified with the poet, but is dramatised, usually ironically, through his or her own words'. The Companion goes on to note that the Victorian poet Robert Browning was especially adept at this form (Browning's **My Last Duchess** - which will feature in a forthcoming *The Art of Poetry* book - is one of his finest dramatic monologues). The key ideas here are that we have a character speaking, not the poet, and that irony is a key device in dramatic monologues. In particular, there is usually an ironic gap between what the central character says about themselves and what the writer implies. We'll keep this idea in mind when we explore character in more detail.

Still thinking in terms of classification, <u>how else might we classify it</u>? Thematically it's a sort of love poem, albeit a perverse one, and it also has a strong narrative element. It reminds me a little of a parable or a moral fable. Like the story of King Midas, it warns of the dangers of greed. There's something of Ovid's story of Erysichthon who desecrates a sacred grove and is cursed by the

Goddess Ceres to suffer such insatiable hunger that he ends up eating himself. Agbabi's use of religious language of 'forbidden fruit', her monstrous characters and the comeuppance of the greedy man suggests to me that she wanted a sort of mythic dimension to her modern fable or urban myth.

How does the protagonist present herself?

- 'When I hit thirty' suggests her age, especially in conjunction with the reference to 'cake'. However we soon realise that this refers to her morbid obesity. That rather indirect way of telling us her weight might imply some embarrassment or shame at her condition
- She's submissive to the man, at least at first: she 'did/ what' she 'was told' even when it brings her no pleasure; parading herself, she seems to do the man's bidding
- She's treated as an object and a possession, an assembly of parts - a 'belly', 'chins' & 'hips'
- A series of metaphors dehumanise her and express her identity in terms of the pleasure she provides for the male character: 'I was his Jacuzzi'; 'forbidden fruit" 'breadfruit'; 'a beached whale on a king-size bed'; 'a tidal wave of flesh'; 'his desert island'. These images suggest she provides him with comfort, sex and also refuge. The adjective  'beached' is significant too as it emphasises the woman's immobility, which is implicit in all the other images of herself. A 'beached' whale is out of its natural element, trapped, helpless and vulnerable. Without help a beached whale will probably die. Like this woman.
- Metaphorical references to her physical size give way to more direct rhetorical language, such as the repetition of 'too fat to...' The tone is

difficult to determine here. Is the woman ashamed of her condition? Her voice sounds neutral, merely cataloguing events, emotionally detached from her own experience, perhaps even numb. Certainly, though the narration is retrospective, there is a noticeable absence of reflective commentary expressing her thoughts or feelings

- The power dynamic shifts between the characters: 'I allowed him to stroke' implies she has some control. And this raises a troubling aspect of the characterisation of the woman; her apparent compliance in her own abuse. In the next line, for instance, the man says 'Open wide' and he pours 'olive oil down' her 'throat'. The woman is either unable or unwilling to resist. Earlier she had said her 'only pleasure' was the 'rush of fast food' the man feeds her. The monstrous descriptions of her body also come from her own mouth

- The understated, matter of fact tone of the horrific last line: 'There was nothing else left eat' so casually explaining resorting to cannibalising his dead body confirms our sense of growing unease with the narrator as the poem progresses.

This last point takes us back to irony in dramatic monologues. Clearly there is an ironic gap here between what the character is saying and what the writer wants the reader to understand by it. She has in fact been turned into a monster by her abuser, but the question remains to what extent did she have some responsibility for the situation. The poem poses, but does not answer this ethical question.

Why is the poem written in rhymes three line stanzas? Technically three lined stanzas are called 'tercets'? The form reminds me a little of Dante's use of terza rima in *The Divine Comedy* and these gluttonous, dysfunctional characters could, perhaps, be found in a modern version of Dante's outer circles of hell. Agbabi's tercets don't feature the chain rhyme characteristic of terza rima and the rhyme pattern, like the metre, has a roughness & looseness about it. Partly the use of half-rhymes rather than full rhymes help generate a believable speaking voice - Browning masterfully uses full rhymes in *My Last Duchess*, but obscures them with caesuras, enjambment and other devices - but the sounds that don't quite fit together might also suggest the tension in the relationship. The three line structure might also remind us that there are three characters in the poem, the unnamed woman and man and behind them the poet.

Though the poem lends itself to a Feminist reading, the imagery might also interest postcolonial critics. As well as reference to a desert island, bread fruit is mentioned which might suggest a master/ servant, coloniser/ colonised dynamic could be mapped on the man and women in the poem. This reading would suggest that in the end the colonised subject will eventually become too big for the coloniser and lead, therefore, to the latter's inevitable destruction.

Crunching

Crunching a poem is a quick and interesting way of reducing the text to its most significant words. Only one word is allowed per line of the poem. I recommend you have a go at completing this task on your own at first and then compare your crunching with your peers. Through discussion see if you can come to an agreed class crunched version. Then compare your version to mine. I'm not presenting mine as the single correct crunch, but you'd have to work hard to convince me that my choices are wrong...

Of course, the crunching process can be usefully repeated all the way down to the most important few words, or even a single word, in a poem. And it can be easily adapted: Crunching the best lines, or images, crunching through picking out all the nouns or adjectives or verbs, and so forth.

Eat Me crunched:

CAKE – LAYERS – WEIGHT – PINK – EAT – TOLD – WALK – BED – WOBBLE – LIKE – BIG – MASSES – JACUZZI – PLEASURE – FORBIDDEN – BREADFRUIT – WHALE – FLESH – FAT – SHIELD – TOO – ALLOWED – GLOBE – OPEN – WHISPERED – TOP – DROWNED – WEEK – GREED – EAT.

In Edexcel's AS exam students have to answer one out of a choice of two questions. Both questions require comparison of two poems. On each question one poem will be selected by the board; the choice of the matching poem will be left to the students:

e.g. Compare the ways in which poets explore the shift from childhood to adulthood in *An Easy Passage* and one other poem. In your answer you should consider:

- themes
- language & imagery
- the use of other poetic techniques

For ***Eat Me*** the question could ask about male and female relationships or the presentation of the female character. If that were the case, good comparison poems would include *A Leisure Centre is also a Temple of Learning*, *The Map-Woman* and *The Gun*.

Simon Armitage: *chainsaw versus the pampas grass*

<u>What do you make of the title of Armitage's poem?</u> Firstly, it is intended to sound like a sports match or a fight. There's no article ('a' or 'the') at the start which also makes 'chainsaw' sound like a name of a person or a team. If we think of chainsaws and their place in popular culture for just a moment or two we'll soon hit on the notorious horror film *The Texas Chainsaw Massacre*. Chainsaws are serious bits of kit, powerful and dangerous tools that can be wielded as weapons by nutcases in horror films. Powerful and dangerous are not words we would usually associate with the rather flimsy, thin stemmed and fluffy headed pampas grass, as shown below, wafting gently in the wind.

Perhaps you've whiled away some time in a lesson or when waiting for a bus by playing imaginary match-ups. Which would win in a battle between a shark and a crocodile? Would a tiger defeat a lion? Who'd come out on top in a final showdown between Superman and Batman? Would Nigella Lawson take down Mary Berry? In this

game the contestants have to be well matched, otherwise there's obviously no fun in the speculation and not much of a fight. In pitching a deadly weapon, armed with rotating sharp serrated teeth propelled by a powerful motor incongruously against some defenceless wavy grass, Armitage makes the battle seem comically one-sided, like Superman vs. Mary Berry. As the first line of the poem acknowledges, 'It seemed an unlikely match'. Inevitably the grass will be wiped out, quickly and easily. Or so we are encouraged to think.

Notice that the poem's speaker is not included in the title: It is not *Armitage & the Chainsaw versus the Pampas Grass*. This adds to the sense that the chainsaw is a distinct character in the poem, acting almost autonomously, with a will of its own. It also excuses the speaker from responsibility for the anticipated carnage to come.

If I were teaching this poem, before reading the poem at all, I'd take some of the lines describing the chainsaw and present these to the class and ask them to speculate about who or what is being described. The same exercise could be done with the phrases describing the pampas grass. A third list would indicate the role of the speaker and their feelings about what they're doing. Students could then try to imagine what would happen when these three agents are brought together in the poem. Alternatively the class could be split into groups each given one of the following lists (obviously without the titles!):

The Contestants: 1. Chainsaw

Here are some of the key phrases used to personify Chainsaw an active agent in the poem's narrative:

- Grinding its teeth
- Knocked back a quarter-pint
- Lashing out at air
- Bloody desire
- Its grand plan

- Swung/ nose-down from a hook
- Instant rage
- Perfect disregard
- Sweet tooth/ for the flesh
- Flare

- Gargle in its throat
- Rear up
- The hundred beats per second drumming in its heart
- Seethed

The Contestants: 2. The pampas grass

- Ludicrous feathers
- Taking the warmth and light
- Stealing the show
- Dark, secret warmth
- Riding high
- Severed
- Mended
- Plumes
- Sunning itself
- Swooned
- Its nest
- Wearing a crown
- The fringe

The Contestants: 3. The poet speaker

The speaker may present themselves mainly as an observer in this comic epic battle, but, obviously, they are not neutral or passive, as the following verbs and phrases illustrate:

- Trailed
- Walked back
- Clipped them together
- I let it
- Felt
- Threw
- Dabbed
- Raked
- Looked on
- Fed it out
- Flicked the switch
- Dropped the safety catch
- Lifted
- Touched
- Poured
- Ripped
- Drove
- Left it

Pulling all the phrases describing the chainsaw together in this way should help to highlight how it is presented as a sort of murderous villain. In fact, the chainsaw is rather like Mr Hyde (pictured below) from Stevenson's Gothic novella, **The Strange Case of Dr Jekyll and Mr. Hyde**: Barely contained

 anger, held on a short fuse, is signalled by 'grinding its teeth' and by 'seethed'. Dynamic verbs suggest the capacity for sudden, frantic, dangerous action, 'knocked', 'swung', 'flare'. The last of these verbs, of course, also suggests fire. Like a horse, the chainsaw, out of control, might 'rear up'. Other words signal murderous, possibly cannibalistic appetite: a 'sweet tooth for the flesh', 'bloody desire'. A lust for violence is indicated, even for senseless, ineffectual, mindless violence: 'lashing out at air'. But this violence can be also directed; there is a malign intelligence at work, a 'grand plan' and a 'disregard', perhaps for law or morality. Crucially, the chainsaw also seems as much a danger to the man wielding it as it is to the pampas grass.

Thinking of Mr. Hyde might lead us in the direction of a <u>psychoanalytic reading</u> of the poem, i.e. that the Chainsaw embodies the poet's subconscious desires. The speaker of the poem inhabits, after all, two separate perspectives; that of the character who wielded the chainsaw and tried to torch the stump as well as the reflective one, looking back at the experience, wryly observing his own foolish actions. This double identity, as participant and observer, is reflected in the verbs above. One phrase, in particular, links the man to the chainsaw: Just as the power tool had 'lashed' out at air' later in the poem the speaker describes himself using the saw as ineffectually: (it was) 'like cutting at water or air with a knife'.

The man's entrance into the poem is delayed until the second stanza, as if he is playing second fiddle to the main character, the chainsaw. But, in the fourth and fifth stanzas, the emphasis shifts to his actions. Look, for instance, at the number of uses of the first person pronoun here. The most disturbing action of the poem takes place in this stanza: The man 'lifted the fringe', 'carved' at and 'ripped into' the hidden centre of the plant, its 'dark, secret warmth'. Transgressive, excessively violent, penetrative action gives way to obsession as the man repeatedly 'cut and raked'. Then he wants to 'finish things off'. The double perspective of insider and outsider is apparent in the emotive language employed do describe both the man's action and its effect on the plant. In addition to the examples cited above, the cutting is presented as a beheading; he 'docked a couple of heads'. The man also seems to get carried away with his destructive power, to be enjoying it; 'this was a game'. Three emotive verbs 'severed', 'felled' and 'torn' are used in close proximity to describe what he does to the grass, all of which can be applied to human beings, especially to limbs severed and soldiers felled in battle.

The poem is structured on antithesis and the pampas grass is presented as an opposite to the chainsaw. Whereas the details of the chainsaw cohere into a pretty definite, voracious and villainous image, the pampas grass is harder to imagine as a single character. The feathers, plumes and nest, for instance, suggest a bird, the theatrical showiness of which might make us think of a peacock. But there's something comical too, its feathers are 'ludicrous', and it 'swoons', something heroines used to do in black and white films. Perhaps there's something of the diva or an old fashioned show girl too in its self-indulgence and greed for warmth and light. 'Riding high' and 'wearing a crown' could fit with this interpretation. Whereas the chainsaw is full of destructive intent, the grass is presented as if sun-bathing, as relaxed and blissfully unaware of the coming violent attack.

It is clear is that the conflict in Armitage's poem is between potent, active male forces (the man, the chainsaw) and a seemingly passive and fragile female force, embodied in the pampas grass. If you're not convinced of this gendered reading, look up the word, 'swoon'; most definitions stress that this verb describe an apparently uniquely female form of fainting brought on by the close presence of an attractive man! Golly!

As we have already emphasised this male vs. female/ man & machine vs. nature fight appears to a preposterous mismatch. However, despite all the violence inflicted on it by the man and the chainsaw, despite all the cutting and docking and slicing and carving and burning, after just a few weeks the pampas grass triumphantly mends, resurrects and re-grows itself:

Tips/ sprang up from its nest...wearing a new crown.

And, in contrast to this bursting, exuberant fertility, man and chainsaw are rendered passive, impotent and redundant.

Featuring a man in relation to nature, thematically Armitage's superficially comic narrative prose poem has something in common with Romantic poems such as Wordsworth's **Nutting** and Shelley's **Ozymandias**. In *Nutting* the young poet chances upon an untouched scene of natural beauty and then senselessly ravages it. In Shelley's poem a speaker happens upon the ruins of a statue of the mighty Pharaoh surrounded by a seemingly endless desert. On the pedestal of the statue are the words 'Look on my works, ye mighty, and despair', a self-

aggrandising statement that is immediately undercut by the statue's location where only 'the lone and level sands stretch far away'. In other words, the works of man are pitiful and puny when set against the immense power of nature and time. (For a detailed examination of Shelley's poem see **The Art of Poetry, volume 1.**)

In Armitage's poem, which I'd like to call Domestic Romantic, the field of conflict between man and nature has shrunk from a desert to a back garden, and man has now created powerful, destructive tools to help him in his fight to control nature. But the outcome is the same; time and mother nature defeat man and machine. This is the truth the reflective speaker of the poem realises and that, as a destructive agent in the poem, he had foolishly forgotten.

Crunching

The officially correct, utterly indisputable, absolutely unarguable version of Armitage's poem crunched is as follows:

MATCH – GRINDING – DARKROOM – HATCH – KNOCKED – JUICES – ACROSS – DRY – GULP – HEAT – WRECKAGE – SPIDER'S – I – GARDEN – POWDER – FLICKED – COUPLED – GUNNED – RAGE – LASHING – MOOD – TANGLE – BLOODY – FLESH – PLAN – REAR – FLARE – HEART – THROAT – FEATHERS – PLUMES – SUNNING – SHOW – SPEARS – SLEDGEHAMMER – NEED – LEVER – OVERKILL – EXIST – SWOONED – DISMISSED – GAME – CARVED – PLANT-JUICE – SECRET – WORK – SEVERED – DEAD – CUT – STUMP – EARTH – FINISH – DROVE – CHOKED – MENDED – KNIFE – POURED – MATCH – LEFT – NEW – SPRANG – CROWN – EGYPT – MOON – SEETHED – MAN-MADE – TIME – FORGET – PERSIST.

Agree entirely? Good.

Other poems that examine human interaction with nature include *The Gun*, *The Lammas Hireling*, *Giuseppe* and *History*.

Ros Barber: *material*

Look at Barber's poem on the page. <u>What strikes you about how it is arranged?</u> To me in looks very tidily regular and well ordered. Nine stanzas, each eight lines long, follow the same cross rhyme pattern, so that the second and fourth lines rhyme with each other. This pattern is then neatly mirrored in the second half of each stanza, so that the sixth and eighth lines also rhyme with each other. Many of the stanzas comprise one sentence and almost all finish at the end of a sentence with a definite full stop. Listen to the poem and you'll notice the metre is regular too; iambic tetrameter ticks away steadily throughout the poem with very few trips, hiccups or variations. A pleasantly neat sonic and syntactical effect is thus created and sustained from stanza to stanza, making each one sound rounded off, satisfyingly complete.

Examine the language of the poem (sometimes called the diction) and you'll find nothing shocking or badly behaved there either. There are no extravagant or fanciful metaphors or potent rhetorical devices, no exotic sound effects and few showy or erudite words ('lassitude' might perhaps be an exception). Nor do words smash together in explosive, original or surprising combinations to generate semantic fireworks. The poem's language does not draw attention to itself. Like its form and structure, it is exemplary in its well composed, unostentatious orderliness.

How do you feel about this trimness and tidiness? Is it to be admired for its craftmanship? How might it relate to the poem's title and themes? Is all this repeating of strict patterns a little excessive, even oppressive, perhaps? We'll come back to that thought at the end of this essay.

Imagine a class of perfectly behaved, neatly dressed, quiet, biddable children. In this dream class is one child who is loud, scruffy and badly behaved. When there is so much that is so well ordered deviations to the norm tend to stick out. In Barber's poem there are just a few disruptive elements. For example,

 in the fifth stanza the second line end word 'foot' does not rhyme with its pair word 'butcher'. But that's a minor deviation. Compared to its polite peers,

Stanza six is almost a delinquent: Not only does it have an extra ninth line, thus throwing the rhyme scheme out of joint, but its second and fourth lines do not rhyme either! ('talons' & 'piano'). If that wasn't enough already, it's also composed of two sentences (mind you, so are about half of the stanzas, so that's not that rebellious). And, and, stanzas five & six are the only stanzas which share a sentence between them and are thus linked by enjambement.

Clearly there's something going on in the middle of this poem. <u>The question is what?</u>

A cynical student might suggest that the poet was just unable to keep the form going and couldn't think of a rhyme for 'talons' (though 'balance' quickly springs to mind in this context). Perhaps the cynic is right, but it's more productive to assume that writers are masters of their craft and as marked a deviation as an inclusion of an extra line quite deliberate. Broadly this is the middle section of the poem, the hinge point where attention will turn away from the mother and the lost world of which she was part to focus on what her daughter has inherited from her. Perhaps the losing of tight control on the

regular pattern foreshadows the daughter's difficulty in following her mother's fixed example. This section of the poem is also about loss of a once familiar and predictable world, of the local greengrocer whose name you knew and the friendly butcher and the Annual Talent Show. A little emotional wobble in the form seems therefore appropriate here.

The central image of the poem is a **metonym**: The old fashioned handkerchief represents the mother and a whole way of life. Noticeably, the speaker's mother behaves in the same conventional, collective way as other women, waving hankies out of trains, using them to mop tears and whip away rouge, always prepared for emergencies with a hanky up her sleeve. In comparison, the narrator has not been able to follow the orderly and conventional pattern of behaviour set by her mother:

There's never a hanky up my sleeve.

And instead of watching her children perform, the speaker focuses on her own creativity, writing a poem, keeping her children happy by sticking them in front of the TV. Clearly she's not the mother her mother was. Guilt creeps in with 'I raised neglected-looking kids'. But the speaker rallies. Despite feeling sorrow and loss for the 'soft hidden history' the handkerchiefs embodied, she decides she can 'let it go' and her 'mother too, eventually', though, that small pause is, of course, telling. The poem ends with a witty pun leading back to the title:

This is your material
To do with, daughter, what you will.

As well as the physical material of the hanky, this refers, of course, to the material of her life which she can turn into writing material. Such witty touches are a feature of a poem that might be categorised as light verse. Indeed with its lightly satirical social commentary and self-deprecating style, Barber's poem has something in common with the work of John Betjeman or a Movement poet, such as Philip Larkin, in his gentlest mode. Other examples of wittiness include the idea of there being so many hankies stuffed up sleeves ('as if she had a farm up there') that they must have fallen in love and mated to produce 'little squares'. Or the notion that male children were given larger handkerchiefs for Christmas because 'they had more snot'.

Radical avant-garde poets would probably be appalled by the idea that a poem could be constructed around as mundane a subject and written in such a neat, well-made form. But modern poets often pay special attention to the apparently small and insignificant. Barber uses a hanky as a gateway to writing about her mother, their relationship, her own sense of herself as a mother and of how society has changed, for better and worse, over time. Indeed, the poem argues that even small changes in behaviour can have major, large scale effects; the loss of the hanky triggers, eventually, the 'shuttered the doors of family stores'.

Back to the question we posed about whether the poem's pervasive tidiness.  To me, this seems a bridge between the poet and her mother. Though the poet's behaviour as a mother might have fallen short of the conventional example she was set, she is a match for her mother in the neat orderly arrangement of words on the page. Indeed, it's not too fanciful to suggest that those tidy stanzas visually look like little pocket squares. Total uniformity, however, would have been oppressive. Hence that deviant stanza six.

Crunch Time

QUEEN – HANKY – PAPER – GARAGES – WAVING – GRIEF – MATERIAL – SLEEVE – CARDI – LACE – EMBROIDERED – SPITTLED – OUT – FARM – LOVE – MATED – NEVER – PRESENTS – SETS – PONCE – NAFFEST – BROTHERS – MALE – SNOT – CLOSED – GIRDLES – HOMELY – MALLS – DEMANDED – BOILING – STORES – DIED – LOSS – GREEGROCER – CAN – HISTORY – EXTRA – FISHMONGER – YOLKS – CRABE – DANCING – TALONS – TAUGHT – PIANO – STEP – TALENT – FENCING – WHIP – SMUDGE – NOSTALGIA – INNOCENCE – TEN-BOB – KILLED – ME – BUY – EAT – COMMIT – NEVER – NEGLECTED – STRANGERS – FORBIDS – BAG – PACKS – MISS – HIDDEN – GO – EVENTUALLY –DIED – TISSUES – COMPLAIN – DISPOSABLE – MATERIAL – WILL.

With the relationship between mother and daughter at the heart of _**Material**_ it links with _**Inheritance, Genetics**_ and _**The Map-Woman**_. Formally, its use of regular form could be compared interestingly with _**Balaclava**_.

Eavan Boland: *inheritance*

<u>What would you say you've inherited from your parents and grandparents?</u>
Perhaps the elegant shape of your nose, your eye colour or your uncommon
academic ability. Maybe your interest in poetry. We may inherit DNA and

 material goods, but we also pick up less tangible things
from our parents, such as attitudes and values. Eavan
Boland's quietly contemplative poem explores what we
inherit from others either deliberately or by accident.
Only she's a bit more specific than that; what interests
the poet here is what is passed on from women to
women, from mothers to daughters. Fathers are

significantly absent from the poem.

Inheritance is written in the first person in an open, conversational style. The
free verse form fits the idea of 'wondering' aloud; it is as if we are being given
intimate, privileged and direct access to the poet's thoughts. The absence of a
metre ticking away through the poem or a rhyme scheme combines with the
long enjambed lines to generate the sense of unhurried calmness and
contemplative mode. Boland also eschews grand or showy poetic devices.
Conventional, inherited features of poems, such as figurative language are,
like men, noticeably absent from *Inheritance*. Rather, like Ros Barber's, in
Material, the language is literal and concrete, composed of ordinary, everyday
words. If all poems can be placed somewhere on a continuum between two
linguistic poles, as illustrated below, Boland's poem is much closer to the left
than to the left hand side.

Flattening   **Blossoming**
into   ....   **into**
prose   **metaphor**

As an Irish writer and a poet at that, and a female poet in particular, Boland

must have been very conscious of her poetic inheritance and especially the giant shadows of W.B.Yeats and Seamus Heaney. Indeed in her essay collection, *Object Lessons*, Boland wrote about how as she had to work hard to find and express her own voice as a female poet both within, but also against, an inherited male tradition. For, at the start of her career in Ireland the phrase 'female poet' was viewed almost as an oxymoron. Yeats's poetry is full of esoteric symbols and is generally written in a highly poetic, bardic and sonorous mode. Among other things, Heaney's work is characterised by his ability to capture the quiddity of the physical world in rich, sensory soundscapes. Paired down, literal and conversational, predominantly Boland's poem is written in as markedly different in style as possible from these two male heavyweights. Arguably it owes its conversational form and accompanying contemplative tone, though, to the Romantic poet, Coleridge who pioneered this form in a series of poems, including ***Frost at Midnight***. Read in this intertextual light, the line 'the ground I stood on was never really mine' has a self-referential, literary resonance. Boland sees herself as literary migrant or interloper in this territory.

This is not to say, though, ***Inheritance*** is entirely devoid of more lyrical or poetic language. As Boland said, she writes within as well as against tradition. Hence the reference to a specific place name 'Three Rock Mountain', a place itself that locates the poem in relation to a sublime, natural environment, recalls the real, named

settings in Yeats' poem. Perhaps there is something Yeatsian too in the lyrical wistfulness of the descriptions of light, 'the blueness in the hours before rain, the long haze afterwards'. Compared to land, water is obviously fluid, it moves about and it is not fixed. 'This is an island of waters' is also metaphorical and connects Boland's personal feelings and the poem's fluid form to unfixity as a broader national condition. But, overall, such self-consciously poetic language is the exception in this highly disciplined poem.

Much more common is a more direct, powerful, declarative mode. For example, the explicit socio-historical commentary from a feminist perspective of the description of Ireland having a 'history of want and women who struggled/ to make the clothing which was all they had/ into something they could leave behind'. In these resonant lines Boland moves outwards from her own specific, individual experience and places it in a wider context of inheritance of struggle and sacrifice. She is as interested in what she has inherited from this context as she is in what she will be able to pass on to her daughters.

As noted, fluidity is embodied in the form of the poem. Indeed almost every line is a different length. Some are very short; the shortest is just three word long; others stretch out to the margins of the page and flow on through enjambement to succeeding lines. Movement is central to the poem's concluding stanza: Having moved outwards, the poem ends with a switch back inwards into the personal. This movement is also out of the present and into the past. Beginning with the conversational phrase 'but then again', Boland recalls a time when her child was sick with a fever and how, in caring for her child, she seemed to perform a kind of miracle: 'I held my hand over the absence of fever'. It is 'as if' she 'knew the secrets of health and air'. That casual, emphatically repeated phrase, 'as if', is crucial to the meaning. In fact, the impression that the poet has magically cured her child is false. The fever has gone, but not as a consequence of the mother's action. Hence the final sentence of the poem, 'I must have learned that somewhere' is deeply ambiguous and ambivalent.

What, exactly, has the poet learned?

On the positive side, to care for her child with great tenderness and devotion, 'I stayed awake, alert and afraid...when dawn came'. On the negative side, that she has inherited the realisation that she is, in fact, powerless, that, as a mother, all she is left with is helpless worry. And the realisation too of a inherited tendency to imagine you have special knowledge 'secrets', a tendency to Yeatsian mystification, to an irrational, superstitious mentality that misrepresents reality. A mixed inheritance indeed.

The poem's fluid form, its refusal to be pinned to any set repeating pattern, suggests that though we may be influenced by the culture in which we have lived, by our own personal past and by the examples of others, we also have some freedom to go things our own way, as Boland, one of the foremost poets of her generation, male or female, has done.

Crunch Time
The poem crunched:

WONDERING – DAUGHTERS – VIEW – MOUNTAIN- HAZE – MINE – GENERATIONS – FLUID – WATERS – HISTORY – NOHTHING – LEAVE – LITTLE – SHAWL – KNITTED – IMITATE – CRAFTS – NEVER – AFRAID – SICK – ABSENCE – SECRETS – IF – SILENCE – LEARNED.

Thinking in terms of form, **_Inheritance_** could be compared with other free verse, reflective poems, such as **_History_**. Gendered readings would link it with **_Material_**. Other poems about relationships with parents and children include **_To my Nine Year Old Self_** and **_Genetics_**.

Sue Boyle: *a leisure centre is also a temple of learning*

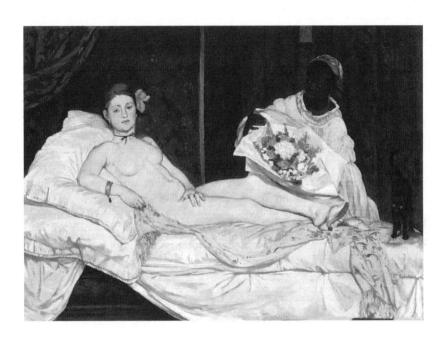

The painting above is by the French Artist, Edouard Manet. When it was first exhibited in 1865, the painting, called **Olympia**, was deeply shocking and highly controversial, not, as we might suppose, because of the female nudity it depicts, but rather because of the unabashed and frank way in which the woman looks back at us looking at her. The effect of this is to make the viewer uncomfortably aware of our own act of looking and the power imbalance between the exposed subject and us, the unexposed audience. Various details, such as her exotic robe and the orchid in her hair, signal that the woman was a prostitute, a fact that obviously added to the painting's capacity to shock its original audience.

How does Boyle's depiction of a female nude differ from Manet's? Does it matter that the artist in Boyle's case is a woman, not a man? If so, why?

Similarities:

- Obviously in their different mediums, both the poem and painting depict a female body
- The two works both present a frank, un-prudish and detailed depiction of their subject
- Although neither artist appears in their poem – both in fact present themselves as onlookers – their presence is suggested by Manet's woman looking out of the picture and by the introduction of the pronoun 'we' at the end of Boyle's poem. In this way, both artists make us, the viewer/ reader, aware of ourselves as spectators and of the act of spectating itself
- Both works have a shock element. In Manet's it is the woman's stare and occupation; in Boyle's it is the new perspective suddenly revealed by introducing the other women as a Greek tragedy-style chorus

Differences:

- The key difference is that the woman in Manet's painting is aware of the viewer/ painter and confronts our gaze steadily and evenly. In contrast the young woman in Boyle's poem is entirely oblivious to the prolonged scrutiny of her nakedness. And this lack of awareness is part of the poem's point
- Boyle's perspective is a female one; Manet's is male. Though the young woman is described by the poet in lyrical and sensual detail as an aesthetic object, I don't think there's anything voyeuristic or pornographic here

- The feminist film critic, Laura Mulvey, coined the term, **the male gaze**, to describe the way visual arts are most often constructed from a male perspective, a perspective which is normalised and hence unacknowledged. In other words, the term refers to the fact women are most often objectified in film, television, advertising by being presented through male values and attitudes. Some literary critics have found the idea useful for examining the presentation of female characters and experience, particularly in terms of literature from the past. Presented outstretched and exposed on her bed for our contemplation, *Olympia*, is constructed through a male perspective. Seen in a comparatively desexualised context of a leisure centre, the young woman in Boyle's poem is presented through a female gaze, but also, crucially, an experienced perspective

- Whereas Manet aims at a photograph-like verisimilitude, Boyle constructs her subject through both close, factual observation of physical details and through a series of imaginative, exotic similes.

The Young Woman

Boyle's subject is described through cataloguing parts of her 'beautiful' body, through her actions and 'dreamy abstractedness' and, as we have noted, through a series of similes. So, we have reference to her muscles, her bone structure her breasts, her throat and so forth. Verbs outline her ritualistic cleansing actions and her self-occupied state of mind: 'showered'; 'applies cream'; 'move'; 'spray perfumes'; absorbed'. Most significant, though, is the figurative imagery: The young woman is described as 'honey coloured' implying sweetness and a taste we can consume. She is also: 'Lithe as a young leopard', 'her breasts' look as though they have been 'sculptured sand from a warm wind', her 'secret cleft' is as neat as a 'charlatan's moustache'. Her hands move 'like a weaver's', her thighs are like 'willow', her head tilts like a 'bird' and her hair is compared to a 'waterfall'. Combined what do these images suggest about her particular type of beauty?

The leopard image implies elegance, sleekness, but also, perhaps power and danger. The image of warm sand connotes gentleness and softness. The movement of her hands suggests skill and suppleness. The image of the 'listening bird' suggests delicacy. The waterfall image, and 'whistle clean' quality of her hair, implies abundance and exuberant energy. Indeed most of these images connect the woman to aspects of nature that are conventionally seen as beautiful. If this leisure centre is a temple, here is its deity, a Goddess of beauty, perhaps of love, like Aphrodite, or Venus, famously depicted below by Botticelli.

Temples are also, of course, places of worship. Who or what is being worshipped here?

After the long, loosely structured, enjambed lines of the first three stanzas there is a noticeable concentration of attention in the second half of the poem. Both the poem's form and technique tighten accordingly. The fifth stanza begins the process, but it really accelerates in the proceeding one: Picking up the opening image of honey, the stanza starts with a very short line, 'A bee could sip her'. Similes concentrate into metaphors: The idea of consuming the woman is developed in another sensual metaphor; she is food as well as drink: 'she is summer cream slipped over raspberries'. At this moment of maximum almost entranced concentration, there is a sudden tonal shift, as the poet and the other onlookers make their belated appearance in the poem. The straightforward factual language of 'she is much younger than the rest of us' switches away from our lingering focus, snapping the poem's aesthetic trance. If the poem were a film, the long unbroken sweeping close-up of the woman and her ablutions is followed by the camera pulling back to reveal characters who, until this moment had been invisible, but nevertheless present in the scene. And significant too.

The mood of the poem suddenly darkens. Single isolated, end-stopped lines build anticipation. <u>Why should she look around?</u> Because, if the other women are the chorus, we are now in the world of Greek Tragedy, first implied by the reference to a 'temple of learning'. The on-looking women, embodying the perspective of experience, know what this beautiful innocent does not, how the action will pan out over the inevitable course of this narrative. Indeed they are living proof of the inexorable effect of time on youthful beauty, however much it is pampered and cherished. Dramatic irony works against the young woman as we, the readers, too know what she, cocooned in her self occupation, apparently does not.

Boyle's title hints at a light comic poem. And there is something comical in this scene of the blissfully unaware, perhaps rather narcissistic young woman being scrutinised by the older poet. But there's a bit of a chill in the air too. The poem ends, after all, with a warning.

Crunch Time

The poem crunched:

HONEY – ABSORBED – TONED – SHOWERED – GENTLE – LEOPARD – BREASTS – CLEFT – DREAMY – LOVED – HANDS – KISSPOINTS – THIGHS – BIRD – WATERFALL – SIP – CREAM – SHOULD – CHORUS – NEXT.

Agree? Of course you do.

Phaedra (1880) by Alexandre Cabanel

With its sustained concentration on a single character, **_A Leisure Centre is also a Temple of Learning_** could be compared with **Material**. Specifically female experience is also the centre of **Inheritance, Eat Me** and **The Map-Woman**. The Blakeian theme of innocence and experience links this poem to **To My Nine-year old self.**

John Burnside: *history*

There's a curious pattern in Burnside's poem that is so insistent in can only have happened by design. Right from the get-go many of the phrases are arranged in patterns of two: The sand and the smell of gasoline; the tide 'far out' and 'quail-gray'; the people 'jogging' or 'stopping to watch' and the planes; the planes that 'cambered and turned'. The pattern is there in the nouns - sand, smell, people, planes - as well as in the verbs or verb phrases as well as in the adjectives. Not convinced? Okay, now you've asked for it:

Nouns	Verbs	Adjectives
The news and the dread	The drift and tug	Captive and bright
The speaker and Lucas	Scarcely register,	Nerve and line
Shells and pebbles	scarcely apprehend	
Kinship or given states	Gazed upon and	
The world and our dreams	cherished	
The wind and the shore		
Gravity and light		
Distance and shapes		
Silts and tides		
Rose or petrol blue		
Jellyfish or anemone		
Light and weather		
Toddler and parent		

There that's proved it, I hope. And there will be more examples. Look, for instance, at the word 'Today'. Having established this insistent pattern of twoness we might then wonder at its signficance, particularly in relation to the poem's title. Before we do that, we'll just comment on another feature this systematic process foregrounds; how dominant nouns are in this poem, especially concrete ones. Action is comparatively scare - verbs are few on the ground and those present are reflective, not dynamic ones. This is a poem, then, composed of things – and those things are generally presented starkly, without the decoration or modification of adjectives.

Back to the significance of this pattern. As the relationship of the grand, abstract title to the specific concrete subtitle inidcates, this mediative, seemingly loosely structured poem sets small apparently insignificant details of personal history against the backgroup of world-changing global events, in particular the 9/11 terrorist attacks on the United States. The poem also has a double perspective; it is comprised of close observation of a particular place and all its distinct components, i.e. the poet's gaze is turned outwards. But it is composed too of philosophical reflection, in which the poet makes his thinking the poem's subject. World wide

and personal events, outer and inner experience, innocent childish and adult perspectives, Burnside's poem is constructed upon these antitheses.

How does the poem's form relate to its theme?

The sense of movement created by the free verse form seems to embody the poet navigating his way between the binary poles of antitheses. He is navigating the space 'lost between the world we own/ and what we dream about'. The path is uncertain and he is unsure of his steps. Hence stanzaless lines shift about, starting and ending at different points. Some are very long and almost make it right the way across the page, others are much shorter; the shortest is just one word of five letters. The poem is also metreless. So no underpinning pattern appears to regulate its movement. It's as if the ground under the poet's feet is unstable, shifting, uncertain.

Sometimes the lineation suggests the in and out movement of waves on a shore:

        I knelt down in the sand
with Lucas
        gathering shells
and pebbles
        finding evidence of life in all this
driftwork

But even the irregularity isn't stable: At other times, when the poem moves inwards into explicit thinking and reflection, the lineation falls into a more regular pattern. Lines resolve into fixed, more solid stanzas, as in the lines starting with **'at times I think...'** and later on with **'Sometimes I am dizzy'**.

Sentence structure adds to the fluidity of the poem's form and the sense of potential disconnection and fragmentation. The first elongated sentence, with its multiple clauses and pile up of phrases, for example, does not come to the end of its weaving, winding journey and its full stop until over half a page and 21 lines later. Indeed the whole poem is composed of only three stretched-out sentences. Between the isolated adverb of time that begins it – 'today' - and the rest of the sentence this word modifies 'I knelt down in the sand' there are, for example, 13 lines. In between these the reiteration of the word, 'today', followed by another long pause of blankness, makes it seem as if literally no time has elapsed since the first line. Looseness, potential fragmentation, hesitation, silence, are generated too through the use of these blank spaces ably aided by the punctuation. Look, for instance, at the number of hyphens on the first page; there are two more of these uncertain, skittish marks here than there are full stops in the entire poem.

Unsurprisingly, in all this local unfixedness and the global turmoil it mirrors, the poet seeks out images of forces that prevent things from drifting entirely apart, stuff which connects things together securely: The kites are emphatically 'plugged' into the sky; bodies are 'fixed and anchored'; water 'tethers' the people to gravity; the fish are 'lodged' in the tide. At other times the poet himself forges these connections, as in the lines:

Sn**ai**l **shells**, **shr**e**ds** of ra**zorfish**;
Smudges of weed and fl**e**sh on tideworn stone,

Here a run of sonic devices, sibilance and assonance, enhanced by the way, syntactically the phrase 'and flesh' can be linked to smudges or to stone, re-enforces the shared lexical field. Diction and sounds lock together to form a whole.

The ordinary, seemingly stable world can seem suddenly more vulnerable and precious in the light of global disasters. Burnside's poem encourages us to value, connect to and find meaning in what is immediately around us, the

world we can touch and smell and hear and see and our relationships within it. Attend to the delicate, temporal 'shifts of light/ and weather' outside and inside ourselves, the poet suggests. He provides us with an enduring image of how to live in this world and 'do not harm' in the 'toddler', an innocent everyman figure, curious about the world around him. We are all, the poem, implies 'sifting wood and dried weed from the sand', 'puzzled by the pattern'. All we can hope is like another child, Lucas, we can find meaning, 'evidence of life' in 'all this driftwork'.

If that sounds like a conclusion, it was meant to. But it isn't. Burnside's poem doesn't in fact end with the lingering image of the child, but with the parents. Parents are figures of experience, more conscious of the wider world around them and Big scale History surrounding their own histories. The final line of the poem is striking and unexpected because it ends with a single adjective 'irredeemable'. <u>Why do you think Burnside choose this one word</u> rather than a synonym such as 'irrevocable' or 'transitory' or over the two word pattern we have seen so dominant throughout the poem? Clearly the poet wanted a word that carries the moral sense of sinful beyond salvation as well as the idea of being beyond cure or remedy. Recalling T.S.Elliot's use of 'unredeemable' about time in **Burnt Norton**, 'Irredeemable' also contains the sense of time that cannot be recovered. Hence packed into this single word the essential twoness of the poem, its two narratives of personal and global History are finally wielded together.

Crunch Time

I've already implied the poem can be crunched to a couple of key lines; the one about finding evidence of life in the driftwork and the final line. It's a long poem to crunch, so I'm going to miss out a few lines:

TODAY – WE – BEACH – SMELL – TIDE – PEOPLE – WAR – MORNING – TODAY – NEWS – KNELT – LUCAS – FATHERING – EVIDENCE – DRIFTWORK – STONE – THINK – KINSHIP – LOST – DREAM – RAISED – ANCHORED – CONFINED – TETHERS – WATER – READING – TIDES – ROSE – JELLYFISH – CHILD'S – FEAR – LOSING – LIVING – VIRTUAL – REGISTER – APPREHEND – MOMENT – LOCAL – LODGED – INSOMNIA – BRIGHT – HUNG – GOLD – HOME – HUM – PROBLEM – CHERISHED – TODDLER – SIFTING – PATTERN – PARENTS – PLUGGED – PATIENT – IRREDEMABLE.

A poem about identity and the interaction between the personal and public world, <u>**History**</u> could be compared with **To my Nine-Year-Old Self, Genetics** and to **Inheritance.** Although it's not in the *Poems of the Decade* anthology, because it was written almost 150 years agoearlier, an interesting companion piece to Burnside's poem would be **Dover Beach** by Matthew Arnold. I don't think it's possible to write a 'beach' poem in English without being aware of this famous predecessor and, intertextually, Burnside's poem can be read as in dialogue with Arnold's. As well as an end of the land/ start of the sea setting, the poems share a similarly pensive mood and Arnold also uses form to suggest the movement of waves, backwards and forwards. <u>How, though are they different?</u> Arnold's poem laments the loss of the 'bright girdle' of religion biding the world together; <u>what does Burnside find that might take the place of this holding force?</u> Certainly there is a spiritual, quas-religious feel to Burnside's poem – the poet kneels in the poem, he mentions a 'book' of nature and he finishes with something like a creed, but, in the end, it's a way of thinking and being in the world that is offered as hope.

Ciaran Carson: *the war correspondent*

Gallipoli

Google Gallipoli and you'll be able to find the historical context for this poem, including many evocative photographs, such as the one below:

If I were teaching this poem, I'd be inclined to give students the poem without the title or the subtitle and ask them to make an intelligent guess as to what these might be. In fact, the poem's quite long (which sometimes puts students off) and it's so densely jammed with details that it could be split up, so that pairs of students are presented with just one or two stanzas in isolation for close inspection. Each pair could then feedback and suggest when and where the poem is set and what it's about. As each group feedbacks a shared sense of discovery will develop, of fitting the pieces together as the full panorama is slowly revealed. Perhaps this would lead to the penny of interpretation dropping that this is a war scene and one from the quite distant past. An alternative would be to present the poem one stanza at a time to the whole class, asking them to work out what they can about each stanza and writing questions they have about it before moving on and revealing the next stanza.

It's a truism that a picture is worth a thousand words. On the other hand, fans of the radio say it has all the best pictures. Certainly a poet only has words and the pictures he or she can conjure in our heads. <u>So how can poetry convey the true horror of war? How can poetry ever hope to capture a scene as filmic and complex, a sprawling muddle as varied as Carson's poem attempts?</u> Having had a very good go at it, this is a point the poet self-reflexively acknowledges at the end of the poem:

I have not even begun to describe Gallipoli.

This is a gigantic list poem: Carson captures the chaotic, collisions of cultures, the sense of overcrowding and claustrophobic space, the intoxicating smells and flavours, the extravagant costumes and the rancid slum setting by piling together a mishmash of specific details, sense impressions, languages and cultural references into tightly knotted sentences. The place names, for instance, take us from London's Billingsgate market to Dublin to India (Benares) to France (Boulogne) to Sheffield to Italy (Bologna) and so forth. This assembly of different cultures and nationalities is inherent in the composition of the landscape too: There English 'sheds and stalls', 'farmer's yards' and 'chimney stacks' as well as an 'Irish landlord's ruinous estate' as well as gutters from France, arcades from Italy, pagodas from China and 'souks' from Turkey. The impression generated is of giddy, disorientating, dilapidated, disease-ridden, sprawling mayhem.

But there are underlying patterns, counter forces of good order, shaping all this teeming content, helping the reader to navigate a way through:
- The voice of the poet

- The stanzas and their ancillary punctuation
- The rhythm
- The complex rhyme scheme

The voice of the poet is in command

All but the final two stanzas begin with an imperative: 'take' is used four times, followed by 'then', 'dress', (the more militaristic) 'requisition' and 'let'. There's something of the cookery book, or instruction manual, in these series of verbs; as if the poet is showing us how to put all the ingredients together in order to create an extraordinary complex and, frankly, unpalatable dish. This language of control and deliberate intent is used ironically. Who or what would put all these incongruous ingredients together in such a chaotic and deadly way? What's the plan? Who is in charge here? No-one, seems to be the answer. Except the poet.

Order is imposed on colossal disorder by the stanzas

The internal content of each stanza may be an ill-matched mayhem of intercultural details slammed together in a list that's bursting out of metrical constraint, and the entire poem is, indeed, one enormous, sprawling, winding sentence, itself a mega-list that lasts for an extraordinary 50 lines, but the regular stanzas doughtily hold back the pressing chaos. Each stanza is a

solid-looking cinquain and each ends in the same orderly way – like a well drilled troop of soldiers semi-colons hold the riotous material in check. And on closer inspection each stanza also has a distinct, coherent subject: The first four establish a sense of place and atmosphere, the fifth focuses on the eclectic inhabitants, the sixth describes their fantastical costumes the seventh refocuses on locations, the eighth on food and drink. There is a change of tone in the penultimate stanza with the apostrophe 'O', as if the poet is throwing up his hands in despair at the impossible task of capturing this place, addressing the 'landscape' as if it is a deity.

Although there isn't a regular metre, a strong emphatic rhythm runs through the poem, kick started by the opening 'take'.

The subtle, inter and intra-stanza, rhyme scheme imposes sonic order on the interior cacophony. Specifically a sonic bond is forged between the first two stanzas: Each line in sequence in the first stanza is rhymed with each line in sequence in the second stanza, first line with first line, second with second and so on, so that the two stanzas form a stable sonic block. The same pattern is repeated in the third and fourth, but with new rhyme sounds and a subtle deviation in the last two lines where the rhymes cross over. This pattern is securely repeated in the fifth and sixth. There is a greater shift in the seventh and eighth, where intra-stanzaic rhyme is introduced in the second and third lines. Check the rhyme scheme in the concluding pair of stanzas and you'll see that it's scrambled, as if the poem can no longer maintain its hold on such turbulent content. Except that, there still is a pattern and there still are rhymes. We might be moving towards total disorder, but we haven't got there, just yet.

With such crammed density of detail to explore, we need some method to help prioritise. We could focus on how Carson employs a range of sensory imagery to create a multi-dimensional impression. Picking a few examples illustrates the exotic vividness of the poem's visual details: 'glittering', 'as black as tin', 'smoking', 'pink flamingo', 'green cantaloupes'. Adding to this rich mix is aural imagery - 'jangly music' and the 'squawks of parakeets' - and a heady stew of pungent smells – 'the reek of dung and straw', 'smells of rotten meat', 'the stench of pulped plum and apricot' – and tastes – 'garlic-oregano tainted', 'rancid lard', 'sour wine' - and movement - 'tumbledown', 'fishes fly', 'leaking ballast', 'houses teeter', 'linguini twists of souks'.

We might catalogue the poem's linguistic richness, illustrating how its diction is drawn from a wide range of cultures. Earthy Anglo-Saxon monosyllables, 'take', 'sheds', 'stalls', 'reek', 'dung' jostle together with more refined words, derived from Latin: 'labyrinthine', 'elaborate', 'deployed', 'requisition' as well as with French words such as 'sans-culottes', 'pantaloons' and 'cantaloupes' and Arabic words such as 'souk' and 'fez', Dutch words, such as 'knickerbocker', and with more unusual, exotic words, such as 'Zouaves', 'Valenciennes', 'boleros', 'oubliettes', 'Trebizond'. Combining these very different sounding words together creates a soundscape for the poem as intoxicating as the pungent smells of the place.

But, as with Burnside's poem *History*, I think a couple of key images capture in microcosm the most significant aspects of the whole picture:

1. ...**green cantaloupes/ swarming with flies washed down with sour wine**
2. ...**soldiers lie dead or drunk among the crushed flowers**

Both these lines convey the double perspective of the poem. This scene in Gallipoli has an exotic, ragged glamour, even a vibrant, intoxicating beauty.

Green cantaloupes sound exotic and the word 'cantaloupe' itself has a liquidy sonic lushness. Flowers obviously also signal temporal beauty. But these symbols of beauty are crushed. Among them are soldiers who are either pleasurably intoxicated or bluntly dead - the casualness of the phrasing implying a callous disregard for these men by their superiors. And the wine has turned sour, the delicious fruit is infested with flies. Chock-full of corruption, destruction and death, the poem also presents us with a vision redolent of John Milton's capital of hell from *Paradise Lost*. Gallipoli here is an earthy Pandemonium.

Crunch Time

TAKE – GLITTERING – TUMBLEDOWN – REEK – DUBLIN – RUINOUS – PAGODAS – SHROUDS – JUNKS – BLACK – GUTTER – TEETER – SHEFFIELD – IRISH – DESTROYERS – GARLIC – ROTTEN – LABYRINTHINE – TENEMENTS – PARLOURS – SLUM – ZOUAVES – NUBIAN – LINGO- TURBANS – FEZZES – PANTALOONS – PINK – STRANGER – SLAUGHTER-HOUSES – RANCID – JAIL – CHOLERA – SEWERS – DIET – SWARMING – BYZANTINE – CITHARA – SQAWKS – RIDDLED – OURLIETTES – OPIUM – SPIES – FAILING – OFFAL – STENCH – BRANDY – DEAD - BEGUN

Obviously dealing with a historical event, the failure of the allied forces to capture Gallipoli from the Turks, Carson's poem could be compared with **History** and with **Fantasia on a Theme of James Wright**. The sense of the strain to impose order on disorder could link **War Correspondent** to **Material** and, whereas Carson is interested in our socio-historical inheritance from the past, Eavan Boland explores that theme on a more personal level in **Inheritance.**

Balaklava

The most famous poem describing this battle is, of course, Tennyson's *The Charge of the Light Brigade*. Clearly, intertextually, Carson's poem is in dialogue with this earlier account, providing a more measured and sombre version of events. (You can find a detailed analysis of Tennyson's poem in volume one of *The Art of Poetry*). Basically, though, Tennyson's poem turned military disaster into an ultimate heroic sacrifice. His poem is full of exciting action as horses charge, canons thunder, sabres flash and the light brigade smash through the reeling Russian defensive line. The whole poem is propelled by a tremendous galloping rhythm, beginning with the lines 'Half a league, half a league/ half a league onward' and pounding right through to the last stanza:

> **When can their glory fade?**
> **O the wild charge they made!**
> **All the world wondered.**
> **Honour the charge they made!**
> **Honour the Light Brigade,**
> **Noble six hundred!**

Tennyson's poem is a tour de force, sweeping the reader up and carrying us along with its vigorous rhetoric. Entirely absent, however, is any sense of the pain, suffering and death in battle. Nor, indeed, is there any acknowledgement that the destruction of the light brigade was a mistake and a military disaster; instead it's presented as a glorious British defeat.

Compare the following lines from Carson's poem with Tennyson's version:

The skeleton of an English horseman
had tatters of scarlet cloth hanging to the bones of his arms

Or:

Round as shot, the bullet-skull has been picked clean
Save for two swatches of red hair

Metrically, the exuberant, galloping momentum of Tennyson poem has been replaced by a flatness, as if the heartbeat of Carson's poem has almost stopped. The tone is also blankly factual. There is no expression of pity or sorrow. These emotion are left for the reader to fill in.

Famously Tennyson wrote his poem from the comfort of home, using a newspaper report. The Victorian poet had never actually experienced battle. Carson switches the perspective, so that his poem is narrated from within th experience by an anonymous soldier. This soldier is marching over the corpse strewn battlefield after the charge, picking his way among graves that grotesquely reveal 'the uncovered bones/ of the tenants' and 'rotted trappings' and 'half-decayed horses'.

Though we are offered an earthbound, humble perspective rather than the panoramic omniscient one chosen by Tennyson, the soldier narrator does provide a vivid visual picture of the whole scene, and, as in *Gallipoli*, in particular, the elaborate, colourful costumes of the participants, like the team colours of a sports team, are emphasised. Our enemy in the first poem, The

Turks, our ally in **Balaklava**, are dressed in 'dark blue uniforms' that looked 'quite black'. Mounted on white horses, the French 'Chasseurs d'Afrique' wear

'light powder-blue jackets' with white belts and 'scarlet pantaloons'. (Ominously the same colour as that found later tattered on the dead Englishman). The following simile, comparing them to a bed of flowers, is poignant in a number of ways. Firstly, the soldiers might look aesthetic and innocent in their bright arrays, but they are 'bristling with steel'. Secondly, for a modern reader, the image suggests the scattering of poppies to honour the fallen. Carson underlines this notion in the succeeding line. Like the detail of the missing buttons on the jackets of the dead and the 'buttoned up' jacket he's wearing, the image of 'poppies red as cochineal' foreshadows our narrator's probable fate.

The reference to smells, the 'delicate perfumes' of the 'crushed springy flowers' mixing with the sweat of men and horses, also recalls the first poem. The idea that helpless nature is crushed by the forces of war is more developed here. And, while, the rhythm is less emphatic and the poem less packed with teeming, sprawling detail than *Gallipoli*, there is a similar ordering of experience through the form and rhyme scheme. *Gallipoli*'s cinquains have swelled in *Balaklava* to even more robust eight line stanzas, sometimes called octaves. Ranks of words move purposively across the plain of the page. Long lines almost, but don't quite, reach the edge of the page. There is an even longer sonic delay than in the first poem before a second rhyme clicks into place and locks with its first. Two sets of two stanzas rhyme with military precision, first line to first line, second to second and so on all the way through.

Except that the last lines of the final stanza do not rhyme, instead they repeat exactly the same words 'arms' and 'jacket'. The inevitable implication of this exact repetition is that these soldiers moving over the battlefield are doomed to repeat the past; that their end will be the same as their fallen comrades.

Unlike Tennyson's poem, Carson's does not include any description at battle. With the striking up of the rataplan, it lies ominously, just coming into view, just over the edge of the page.

Crunch Time

TURKS – FLASHED – BAYONETS – BLACK – EN MASSE – SCARLET – WHITE – FLOWERS – RED – SOIL – RUE – COUNTLESS – BOOTS – CRUSHED – PERFUMES – SMELL – ABOVE – PHALANXES – SLAIN – DEADLY – FATAL – SKELETON – SCARLET – BUTTONS – SKULL – REMAINS – GRAVES – UP – HALF-DECAYED – RATAPLAN – SWEPT – BUTTONED.

Julia Copus: *an easy passage*

Used in film and narrative studies, the term *in media res* describes an opening that throws the audience straight into the middle of the action already happening. Copus's unmetred, filmic free verse poem begins in this manner, midway through the story:

Once she is halfway up there

A character is mentioned, as if we have already been introduced to them, and a place, as if we know where 'there' is. The term *liminality* is used in literary studies to describe inbetween states, when things are neither quite one thing nor another. As they are neither night nor day, dawn and twilight, for instance,  are liminal states; similarly, neither dead nor alive, a vampire is a liminal Gothic figure. The fact that the poem starts halfway through and the girl is halfway up suggests Copus is interested in the space in between things and the transition from one state to another. The title of this enigmatic poem, which recalls the phrase 'rites of passage', allied to the fact that the central character is a teenage girl, in addition to the detail that she is 'half in love', added to the fact that she is suspended for most of the poem on the point of moving from the outside to the inside, strengthens this impression.

After the initial establishing of the girl's location, action in the poem is suspended in the manner of a filmic cliff hanger. Copus uses a number of techniques to stretch and hold the moment out and thus to generate tension:

- Our omniscient narrator takes us into the girl's thoughts, 'she knows that...she must keep'

Use of the present tense means we are uncertain of the outcome – perhaps the girl will fall

- Reference is made to the danger and precariousness of her situation, 'the narrow windowsill' and 'sharp drop'
- Description of what she can see from her restricted and concentrated field of vision, 'the flimsy, hole-punched, aluminium lever'
- The first sentence runs for 13 lines, at the end of which she still hasn't actually entered the house: 'In a moment she will...' is in the future tense
- In the following sentences she is still held immobile. Tactile imagery helps us share her physical sensations, 'the asphalt/ hot beneath her toes'
- Authorial intrusion in the form of philosophical reflection slows time: 'What can she know/ of the way the world admits' taking us out of the time of the story into time of the mind
- Cross cuts to other characters: the mother, the factory workers, the secretary, the other girl, arrest the movement of the suspended girl's narrative.

Only in the last sentence of the poem does time start up again, the girl cross the threshold and drop into the house.

Description of the girls

Like icons in religious paintings, the two girls seem radiant, 'lit, as if form within' and are both associated with light, 'shimmering', 'flash'. They are also utterly absorbed in their experience, so that the house 'exists only for them'. Their near nakedness is emphasised by the reference to the 'bikini', to 'tiny breasts' and in the phrase 'next to nothing'. Conventionally nakedness would signify vulnerability, but, despite the precarious predicament, the girls do not seem weak. In fact, in the poem's final simile associates them with powerful explosive weapons: 'like the/ flash of armaments'. Accompanied by this momentous explosion, the girl crosses the threshold (into the house/ into adulthood) completes her passage from one state to another with ease and indeed, 'gracefully'.

Other characters

There are two other female characters in the poem, the mother and the secretary. Both are described as 'far away' from the girls, as if they are in another dimension entirely, far away in experience as much as in space. The mother has not trusted her daughter with a 'key' to the house, which, if we take the act of breaking into the house as symbolising moving from girlhood to womanhood, implies the mother wishes to prevent her daughter from growing up. With her head full of distractions, the secretary seems to stand as an opposite to the girls. They are totally absorbed in the moment as it is happening, whereas the secretary is reading an 'astrology column' trying to find evidence of fate. Rather than acting as a determining agent in her own narrative she is waiting for things to happen to her.

The startling, surreal image of 'long grey eye of the street' suggests an audience or camera watching the girls, making tangible the filmic quality of the poem. The most important fact is that the girls can act unwatched by an outside eye, they are free from its potentially controlling gaze and from social mores. Freed, they can grow up.

The relationship between them

Like characters from a William Blake poem, the girls are presented as

dynamic figures of innocence, contrasted starkly to the experienced perspective of the road's eye, the factory workers and the two other women. The central philosophical question in the poem which appears nearly in the poem's centre, 'What can she know/ of the way the world admits us less and less/ the more we grow', implies that as we get older we lose direct connection with our experience. Thinking about it, reflecting on it, planning alternatives and so forth, we stop feeling it in the present, now. Whereas when we were young, like these two girls, we felt experience more intensely, sensuously and directly, tasted it on our tongues.

Why doesn't the poem have any stanzas?

Throwing light on the decisions the writer made, rearranging the form of a poem is always a potentially interesting exercise. What difference, if any, would it make if Julia Copus had written her poem in a neat series of quatrains, or in an irregular stanza form or, perhaps, in couplets? The fact that the poem is a single unbroken whole is certainly striking. Like a single, sustained, sweeping camera shot, this unbroken form implies that all the poem's content is part of one single picture, one interconnected situation; a whole, in fact. Only with the poem's last line, when everything is changed, will a new situation begin. This is such a major break, such a significant change, in fact, that the poem cannot continue. Indeed, if this poem were a novel, its final line would function like a chapter break. Imagining what happens next, we might be able to write the next poem. Perhaps this new poem could begin with, 'Dropping gracefully into the shade of the house'.

With an unmetred, unrhymed prose poem such as *An Easy Passage* the lineation is crucial. If lineation is not done well, a poem degenerates into prose chopped up, prose merely masquerading as verse. To test the effectiveness of Copus's lineation we should be able to take a few lines at random and examine their design. We might, for instance, consider the fourth to sixth lines. In the first of these the poet obviously wanted a gap between the words 'sharp' and 'drop' for mimetic effect. Rearrange the line, move 'drop' to line four and this effect is tangibly diluted. Similarly, the small pause after 'mind' in the next line makes us wonder, for a moment, what it is she must keep her mind on, taking us into the girl's experience. In the sixth line it is clear that Copus wanted the word 'love' to carry the emphasis achieved by placing it at the end of the line, so that the sentence and the lineation build toward this significant word.

In a similar vein, we might also examine Copus's use of breaks in the middle of lines, a device known technically as caesura. The most emphatic caesura concludes the first sentence of the poem not at the end, but within the line:

...to the warm flank of the house. But first she

Though the girl shares this line with the house, which is itself described here as if it were, like her, alive, she is also separated from its comforting 'warm flank' by the caesura. Hence closeness and distance, connection as well as separation are neatly re-enforced. Notice too how the break at 'she' leaves the girl hanging for a moment at the end of the line, the pronoun waiting for its connecting, reassuring verb, 'steadies'. If you're still not convinced that careful design has gone into the lineation in this poem try examining the rest of the lines to see if you can propose better points at which to start and end them.

The Crunch

HALFWAY – TREMBLING – MUST – NARROW – DROP – LOVE – WAITING – BENEATH – WINDOW - FLIMSY – MOMENT – LEANING – FLANK – CROUCHING – TOES – PETRIFIED – KNOW – LESS – GROW – LIT – EXISTS – ONLY – EYE – TRUST – DRAB – FACTORY – FAR – FULL – PLANS – OMENS – THIRTEEN – NOTHING – STOMACH – GAZE – SHIMMERING – OUTSTRETCHED – SUNLIGHT – ARMAMENTS – DROPPING.

With its Blakeian theme of innocence and experience, _**An Easy Passage**_ links to **A Leisure Centre is Also a Temple of Learning** and **To my Nine-year-old self**.

Tishani Doshi: *the deliverer*

Think about the title for a moment. <u>What are the different connotations of the word 'deliverer'?</u> Clearly the subtitle gives the poem a religious setting and in this light 'deliverer' takes on the sense of Christ, redeemer and deliverer of mankind from evil and sin. The poem is also about childbirth and we talk about delivering a baby. Thirdly, there is Catholic sister in this hard-hitting, laconically expressed poem who rescues the young girl. Lastly, there is the figure of another rescuer, the American mother who saves a girl who might, or might not be, the narrator herself. It seems, at first, that in rescuing the girl the adopting mother is a Christ-like deliverer. However as the poem develops a more complex and uncertain, blurry picture emerges.

The details in the first stanza are starkly brutal. This is a context in which to be dark skinned or female is a form of disability. And to be disabled is to be called that much harsher, more pejorative term 'crippled'. And in such an unforgiving environment unwanted children are 'abandoned' 'naked'. If this were not horrifying enough, one girl is buried up to her neck underground. This girl, it transpires, might, or might not be, our narrator.

Isolated, as if it signals a new beginning, the final line of the first section of the poem appears initially to offer a happy ending to this short, tragic story:

This is the one my mother will bring.

The choice of a star * as punctuation resonates with the religious setting and seems further evidence of a hopeful resolution.

'Bring' is odd, though. <u>Shouldn't it be 'take'?</u> Bring would imply movement to the convent not from it. In which case the second reference to 'my mother' is to a different mother than the first one. Things are already more complex than they first appeared. The first time we came across the word 'mother' in the opening line of the poem we naturally would have assumed that it refers the narrator's biological mother. But, in fact, it seems more likely that it pertains to the adopted mother who is visiting the convent. It would seem odd if this first second mother is also the mother in the American couple, waiting at the gates for their new adopted daughter, as they 'haven't seen or touched her yet'. The next use of 'mother' refers back to the birth mother who not only abandoned her child but 'tried to bury' her, which implies this was the child mentioned in the first section found by the dog. Hence, when we next come across the word two lines later, there is a further blurring of characters. The results is that it becomes all but impossible to distinguish one mother from another. We must assume now that this is the American mother who is crying. Unnerving uncertainly creeps in with the next line, 'feeling the strangeness of her empty arms'. We do not have a distinct, single subject; it could be the mother or the narrator who has this 'feeling' and why are the arms 'empty'? Due to the uncertain use of the word 'mother', is this perhaps a reference to the birth mother's loss? Added to this confusion of multiple possible mothers is the fact that the convent is named after another mother, **'Our Lady of the Light'.**

And who's to say the sister is telling the truth? She is 'telling' a story that

elicits sympathy, but <u>how do we know it is true?</u> It's quite possible in a complex context with a toxic mix of social shame, sin, child abandonment, poverty and adoption into a completely different culture, and nationality, that this is a convenient narrative

hiding a more disturbing reality. Uncertainty is inherent at the start of the girl's life; she only has the story the sister tells to depend on.

Certainly, the third section of the poem suggests the transition into a new life was not as easy as the arrival at the airport seemed to promise. Growing up on 'video tapes' implies a virtual and westernised way of life. Distance from real life is repeated in the choice of the distancing three person voice, if we assume she is writing about herself. If the poet is writing about another girl, then the fact that she remains anonymous 'the girl', creates a similar effect. Worse, the life's also unsettled. The child is 'passed from woman/ to woman'. Notice how the maternal link is also lost; she is not passed from one mother to another mother. Though she has moved into a different life, her personal history exerts a powerful pull on her imagination, implying that she cannot escape the past. Trying to return to her origins, as if there she might discover her true self, is a forlorn exercise. And, instead, of finishing optimistically, the poem ends with grim images of infanticide, a 'heap' of abandoned girl babies. It is as if this original trauma cannot be escaped or left behind. In this way, the poem explores the vexed issue of inter-racial, cross-cultural and inter-national adoption, as well as the complex ways we form a sense of our personal identities.

Postcolonial critics might be especially interested in this poem, with its seemingly stark contrast between two worlds. On the one side we have the apparently benevolent Catholic nuns saving children from terrible fates. The American couple too, who know 'about doing things right' who, from their perspective are also deliverers, are presented on this side of virtue. On other side we have a picture of life in India that is irredeemably brutal and bleak.

Crunch Time

MOTHER – CHILDREN – CRIPPLED – NAKED – GARBAGE – ABANDONED – DOG – POKING – CHEW – MOTHER – PARENTS – AMERICAN –RIGHT – TOUCHED – FETISH – BURY – CRYING – MOTHER – EMPTY – GROWS – PASSED – TWILIGHT – BIRTH – DESOLATE – OUTSIDE – LIFE – PENIS – HEAP – AGAIN.

With its focus on female experience and the complexity of identity **_The Deliverer_** could be linked to **_The Map-Woman_**. Its concern with what we inherit from the past and this shapes our sense of ourselves also connects it to **_Inheritance_** and **_Genetics_**.

Carol Ann Duffy: *the map-woman*

- <u>What different things make us who we are?</u>
  Perhaps our age, gender, nationality, our appearance, values and actions, the ways we speak, our thoughts, our dreams, the choices we make.

- <u>What are the key influences that shape our identities?</u>
  Our family, our friends, school, where we live, the media, social media, our genes.

If I were teaching this poem, I'd be tempted to start with a survery on how we construct our identities. Students would have to rate the influence of various factors, such as the ones suggested above, on, say a scale of 1- 10. Hopefully this would hook their interest in the topic and help them to connect their own experiences to many of the poems in this selection from *Poems of the Decade.* I wonder how highly students would rate the place they grew up as an influence on their sense of who they are. This idea, of course, is the subject of Duffy's poem.

Comprising 13 sturdy stanzas each ten lines long, this is a monumental poem; a form fitting for a character who seems larger than life, like a figure out of a fairy tale, legend or urban myth. Though the regular stanzas are each almost as hefty as a sonnet, there's nothing ponderous about the poem's rhythm. It sets off at a lick and doesn't let up for 130 lines, carrying the reader along with the narrative. Generally the poem trips along in common metre, more technically known as tetrameter. Sometimes this metre shortens to trimeter, quickening into skipping anapaests:

With a dress, with a shawl, with a hat
De de DUM, de   de DUM, de de DUM

This four line, three line pattern slips the poem occasionally into ballad metre, appropriate for a tall tale. At other times the poem lengthens its stride with extra syllables swelling the line into a loose pentameter:

Beloved mothers and wives, the nuns and priests
De DUM de DUM de de DUM de DUM de DUM

These shifts obviously help give a pretty long poem the variety it needs to breathe, but also encode a sense that an exact same pattern does not always have to be followed, that what's gone before will not necessarily entirely dictate what will come after. Within the regular pattern of the repeated stanza form, on a metrical level, we have irregularity, words going their own way.

The rhyme scheme is also irregular. Rhymes don't appear dutifully at the end of lines, but pop up internally from time to time. In the first stanza, for instance, 'town' half rhymes with 'grown', 'up' with 'muff', 'jeans' with 'sleeved', 'tattoo' with 'grew' and, in rapid fire, 'skin' with 'binged', 'thin', 'slimmed' and 'begin'. Again, these sonic echoes and connections help to make the poem lively and engaging, but also signal, like the metre, that things can take a surprising and unexpected twist.

Through describing the unnamed 'map-woman's' tattoos, Duffy is able to outline small town life, as filtered through the perspective of an adolescent. This is familiar, market town, parochial England, with its church, market and coffee house, its local dignitaries and park benches. And it's a small town from the past; instead of a multiplex there's a 'Picture House' showing films from the 1960s and it has trains still powered by 'belching steam'. This is the parochial world the map-woman knows so well that it's become part of her, written on her skin. The word indelible springs to mind, with its double meaning of something we cannot forget and of making marks with a pen that cannot be erased. The tattoo of her home of her town is like a fingerprint, an indelible, unmistakable, traceable key to her identity.

In an out-of-the-way, unremarkable, conventional place like this we can feel that real life, glamour and excitement must happen elsewhere - surely to goodness, it must. We may feel this especially acutely when we're adolescents. Details in the poem express a yearning to get away from the suffocating ordinariness of small town life. In the coffee house 'you' would 'find yourself':

...waiting for time to start, your thin face/ trapped in the window's bottle-thick glass like a fly

In the station even the trains are 'pining' to escape to a life in the big cities, their names listed like a litany: 'Glasgow, London, Liverpool'. The castle on the hill is like a 'stale cake'; the air in the cinema is 'musty'; the bandstand is 'empty'; even the motorway 'groaned'. The sense that the place exerts an oppressive, possibly damaging influence on the woman is also conveyed by the fact that 'the prison and hospital' are described as being 'stamped' on her back and the via the implication that she tries to get it out of and off her skin, to erase its influence: 'She sponged, soaped, scrubbed'.

It comes, therefore, as something of a surprise to discover in the seventh stanza that she has, in fact, escaped and moved down south. And from this first flight she has remained unfettered, perpetually mobile, 'abroad...up  north...on a plane or train...or boat'. Also she is successful; her clothes are luxurious and feminine, 'linen, satin, silk', she rides in a 'limousine', she speaks another language, she has a lover.

Crucially, though, wherever she goes, however far from her home town she strays, 'the map' remains. Intimately part of her, unnervingly close, dangerous even: 'under the soft silk scarf *at her throat*'. Alarmingly personified, it 'knows every knock and cranny' of her body. It is as if the more the woman seeks to deny it, and fly from it, the stronger, more possessive the tattoo grows. Further images personify it:

- **The map perspired**
- **The map seethed/ on her flesh**
- **The map translated everything back**

And it brings her pain, such as her father's house 'pressing into the bone', carrying the ominous sound of 'thumping'. Some sort of confrontation is inevitable.

As I've mentioned, the poem has something of a ballad feel in its metre. This is also evident in the structure of its narrative. Having had the setup of the opening situation and the development as the woman moves away, we now arrive at the climax of her story, signalled by 'So one day'. In the climax of a narrative opposing forces come into open, direct conflict and one, generally is victorious and the other defeated. Replace Harry Potter and Voldemort with the woman and the indelible dark mark of her tattoo. Who's going to win?

The woman returns to where she grew up and finds that everything has changed. And as she sleeps the tattoo shuffles off her skin, 'sloughed/ like a snake's'. Transformation scenes are common in Gothic literature as well as in fairy tales, legends and myths. Often they are emblems of mutability, for the capacity for people to change their identities, however fixed these  might appear. In Angela Carter's collection of postmodernist stories, *The Bloody Chamber*, for instance, lions turn into humans, humans become tigers and so forth. Duffy's description of the metamorphosis scene is wonderfully sensuous. Slithery sibilance, 'the skin of her legs like stockings, silvery, sheer' vividly mimics the sound and feel of the action.

The metre lengthens into appropriately loosening anapaests: 'for the tissuey socks of the skin of her feet'. This first set of images culminate with the brilliantly unnerving 'her sleep/ peeled her'. Brilliant because it implies this action is the working of her subconscious self. Unnerving because it suggests, unaware and vulnerable, she is like a piece of fruit. About to be consumed. The sense of transgression and erotic danger is maintained in the stripping of the woman: Her thong is 'lifted' along with the 'bra of skin from her breasts. It is a relief therefore to read that this magical helper that has stripped her of her outer skin is benevolent.

The woman finds the skin, decisively dismisses it from her mind and in one verb laden, zippy sentence is leaving the old town behind in her rejuvenated wake:

She left it there, dressed, checked out, got in the car

Victory then to the woman and the benign spirits who helped her escape the past. Except that in a final twist, the poem ends by switching focus to under the surface of the happy resolution. As if setting up the narrative for the sequel, **Map-Woman II, the Return of the Repressed**, deep down, like moles or worms, the old town is moving and ominously 'hunting for home'.

The crunch

With such a long poem there's no need to crunch every line, but we'll see how we go:

SKIN – CHILD – COVERED – DRESS – HOODED – GREW – BINGED – PRECIS – HEART – MARKET – CHURCH – SHADOWS – ARTERY – NIPPLE – GRAVES – TEACHERS – MAYORS – FADING – CONFETTI – BELL – WHERE – DIE – START – TRAPPED – FLESH – HURRY – MAP – KNEW – MUSTY - HOFFMAN – SCRUBBED – PRISON – EMPTY – HEADING – WAR – PINING – WAVING – STEAM – KNEW – ANCHORED – DIVE – HOME – NOW – EN ROUTE – BUT – UNDER – BONE – THUMPING – SNARL – GROANED – GIRL – TOSSED – METAIL – CIAO – MIRROR – RUNNING – FACE – UNSURE – BODY – EVERY – PAST – PILED – LIMOUSINE – SEETHED – BACK – LOVERS – LOST – SO – BACK – STALE – CRUMBLED – BATH – WRONG – NEW – STRIPPED – SLOUGHED –SNAKE – SKIN – MATCH – TISSUEY – PEELED – BREASTS – PARENTS – MARK – WOKE – GHOST – SHROUD – LEFT – GLITTERED – ATE – RASH – DEEP – HUNTED.

With its central subject of how identity is formed, **The Map-Woman** can be linked with **Genetics**, **Material** and **Inheritance**. The effect of the past on the present would make an interesting link with **Out of the Bag**, while the supernatural element or urban myth might connect it to **The Lammas Hireling** and **Eat Me.**

Ian Duhig: *the lammas hireling*

This mysterious, supernatural narrative poem lends itself to translation into a film. Have a go at storyboarding your own version. Decide on a suitable setting, soundtrack, comprising music and ambient sound, as well as lighting, camera angles and so forth. Once you've completed this task you might want to compare with the following version: **https://vimeo.com/45341598**

Notice how swiftly the narrative moves through time in the first stanza. We go from the opening 'after the fair' to the magical effect the stranger has on the cattle in two short sentences and just four lines. The sensual simile 'fat as cream' recalls the phrase the 'cream of the crop', signalling the enriching influence of the hireling. What is the effect of beginning the sentence 'then one night' at the end of the first stanza? The caesura in the last line emphasises a distinct break, a sudden change in the relationship between narrator and the stranger. Enjambement facilitates smooth transition from the first to the second stanza and allows Duhig to place the word 'disturbed' in a prominent position at the start of the first line of the second stanza. Hence tension in the poem ratchets up quickly.

The striking image of the wife's 'torn voice' uncannily distorts sound into something physical, tangible. Torn also suggests emotional suffering, loss but also perhaps violence. For some reason we cannot fathom, this hireling has taken on the voice of the dead wife and tormented the speaker out of his dreams with it. Or perhaps it is the farmer who projects his feelings onto what he hears. In any case, a filmic freeze frame then holds the narrative in suspense for a moment:

Stock-still in the light from the dark lantern,
Stark naked but for the one bloody boot of fox-trap

There is a growing sense of mystery and of the uncanny. The physical world is not operating in the ways we expect: paradoxically the lantern is 'dark', yet, light emanates from it. Has the mysterious stranger adopted the wife's voice because he has been caught in the fox-trap? Such a reading would seem to fit with 'torn'. Or is this what the narrator imagines? Why is he naked? Perhaps, he is shapeshifter, like a werewolf or other magical creature, that divests itself of the cloak of human clothing at night to resume its natural form. Nakedness also suggests vulnerability. Moreover the hireling seems to be immobile. <u>Is he a threat?</u> Though the narrative has moved fast, we are now held in this prolonged moment of description - we do not know how the narrative will progress. The speaker might, for instance, feel sympathy. Is there something semi-erotic too in this scene? The stranger has taken the place of the wife as the narrator's companion in his home, brought fertility with him, takes on her voice, and now stands naked and helpless in the middle of the night.

 But, then, unlike the reader, the speaker becomes certain: 'I knew him for a warlock'. The phrase 'to go into the hare gets you muckle sorrow' confirms the idea that the stranger is a shapeshifter, has turned himself into a hare and then been caught in a fox-trap. Or, at least, it confirms that this is what the poem's speaker believes. The proverbial sound of the phrase and the use of the Northern or Scottish dialect adjective, 'muckle' (very much) makes it sound like it is derived from inherited folk wisdom. It's as if this sort of thing – a man metamorphosing or being metamorphosed into a hare and then getting into some sort of fatal trouble – is not that out of the ordinary. We're in a strange, uncertain world in this poem.

Like his mind, the speaker's actions are decisive and definite. Despite all that it has done to bring him good fortune and makes his cattle fertile, as if appalled by the notion that the hireling has somehow taken on the role of his wife, he shoots him straight 'through his heart'.

As with the voice being 'torn', abstract and concrete become uncannily mixed; it is time, the 'small hour' that the speaker fires. In addition to the strange interplay of light and dark, the reference to disturbing dreams and to a shapeshifting 'warlock', another Gothic trope, the moon, is introduced. The appearance of the moon often prefigures transformation in Gothic literature; think, for example, of a werewolf. In this transformation the hireling seems to return to his natural state, developing 'fur', 'like a stone mossing'. This gentle, natural image of metamorphosis is followed by surprisingly tender language. The hireling's head is described as 'lovely' and in another startlingly original visual image, his eyes 'rose like bread'.

The poem's form continues to contribute to the unsettling, fatally transgressive atmosphere. Though the poem is composed in four even and orderly looking sestets, lines start and end in unusual places; in the middle of lines, at the end of them, overlapping from stanza to stanza. It's as if the sturdy form of the poem has been shaken, gone askew, disturbed like the narrator and his dreams. So, the narrative moves on and, at the end of the third stanza, the stranger's body is put in sack which magically grows lighter and by the next stanza it has been dropped off a bridge. So uncanny have the actions been so far that it almost doesn't come as a surprise to read that the dropped sack makes no 'splash'. These final details suggest that, perhaps, the hireling was a figment of the speaker's imagination, or that, at least, the scene in which the speaker shot him was. With its eerie transformation, perhaps the scene late in the house was actually a part of the farmer's dream.

Like the killing of the albatross in Samuel Taylor Coleridge's **The Rime of the Ancient Mariner**, the murder of the mysterious, fortune-bringing stranger brings a curse down on the narrator. He cannot even dream now of his dead wife, and his herd, that was as 'fat as cream', is now afflicted by malign magic, 'elf-shot'. In another surprising development the poem ends with the speaker using traditional Christian, specifically Catholic, language to try to absolve himself. The fact that it has only been 'an hour' since his 'last confession' may convey obsessive feelings of guilt or his desperation to find some way to mend his cursed fortunes. Or both.

Duhig's poem is a strange, beguiling, Gothic folk tale. The poet

leaves the significance of the story for the reader to try to puzzle out. It is like a parable, but one whose meaning is not accessible to outsiders. Perhaps it is a sort of cautionary tale, warning us about how we treat the things in nature we do not understand and the harm we may do ourselves as a consequence of our ignorance. When confronted by the stranger's mysterious behaviour the speaker immediately demonises what he doesn't understand, precipitately jumping to the conclusion that the stranger is a 'warlock'. The title uses the Northern word 'lammas' which is connected to a pagan festival celebrating the wheat harvest. The mysterious stranger takes on the form of a hare, a conventional symbol of fertility. Perhaps then, he is a god of fertility, akin to the Greek God **Dionysus**, a character from myth presenting himself to a host in humble attire, whose transformational magic is misunderstood by the superstitious narrator and killed with his modern man-made weapon, a gun. After all, did this speaker really have to shoot the stranger, who had brought nothing but benefit into his life? You'll have to answer these questions yourself.

What is certain, I think, is that Duhig's poem is wonderfully rich and vivid, it weaves a magic like a charm itself. It is full of memorable images. The American poet Wallace Steven's dictum that **'The poem must resist the intelligence almost successfully'.** It is a great example of what the poet and critic Glynn Maxwell refers to as a 'lunar' poem in his useful book *On Poetry*; a poem that does not give up its meanings easily, but lingers in the mind after reading and haunts the imagination.

The Crunch

HEART – CHEAP – DOTED – CREAM – DOUBLED – NIGHT – DISTURBED – DARK – NAKED – WARLOCK – HARE – WISDOM - HEART – MOON – FUR – LOVELY – BREAD – SACK – DROPPED – ELF-SHOT – CASTING – BLESS – CONFESSION.

Featuring the entrance of something from another dimension into the ordinary world, Duhig's poem could be compared with *The Gun* and to *Giuseppe*. Man's interaction with the nature links it to *Chainsaw versus the Pampas Grass* and with its mythical narrative mode and transformation scene *The Lammas Hireling* could be compared to *The Map-Woman*.

Helen Dummore: *to my nine year old self*

Imagine you're going to write a letter to yourself, from the distant future. Imagine you're in your sixties or seventies or even older. What would you write to yourself? What would you tell you about how your life has turned out? What advice might you give yourself about how best to face life's vicissitudes? Or, if that doesn't appeal, find a photo or small piece of film of yourself aged about five, about the age you would have started school, and write a piece to your younger self, updating yourself on how your life's turning out.

If you do have a go at either letter try to write freely, don't overthink it, just let whatever comes out flow as much as possible. Set yourself the challenge to write continuously for about fifteen minutes. Then try turning your text into a poem. Think of the transformation as a process of distilling or boiling down to absolute essentials. Choose only your best lines. Cut anything and everything you can, without losing sense. Think of yourself as Genghis Khan when you're doing this; be ruthless, cull, hack, obliterate, take no prisoners. Try to create a few holes in the story for the reader's  imagination to fill, make them work things out a bit. Then step back from the butchery, clear away the blood and see what you've got.

As teachers know too all well, there's a danger that once students start A-level English creative writing gets put on a back seat or is sent entirely to Coventry. A narrowing of the type of written responses to literary texts often takes place at this level, with the formal academic essay dominating. Some specifications offer the opportunity for students to try their hand at re-creative writing, which is always a challenging, but fun way of getting inside a text. Taking on the role of the writer, deciding which way to go, choosing what language and devices to use, just keeping the engine of a text ticking over is demanding, akin to climbing into the driving seat of a racing car. And, nearly as exhilarating, maybe. And, however insightful the teaching, encountering every poem in this anthology through the same process of analytical reading would be reductive. Seek out and promote opportunities for creative writing; improving their creative writing will sharpen students' appreciation of writing craft and virtuously cycle back into the rest of the writing they do at A-level. It will also make palpable for them the fact that creative writing is a form of discovery, a way of thinking and of processing our life experience.

In her poignant, reflective and stylistically understated poem, Dunmore, a successful and acclaimed novelist for adults and children, creates a strong sense of her two characters and of the relationship between them. Starting her poem with the second person 'pronoun' she engages the reader in the relationship, placing us in the shoes of a silent addressee; hence we are aligned to the child. The short, stark first line immediately makes us wonder what the narrator must have done. So, straight-off, with minimum fuss Dunmore engages us in the world of the poem.

The nine-year old Dunmore
What are the key characteristics of this silence listener?

Keen to be on the move, she is a fizz of boundless, dynamic energy. She embraces the experiences the world has to offer, revels in the freedom to simply express herself physically. Full of plans, she is interested in anything and everything, easily distracted, creative, entrepreneurial, fearless, vibrant, adventurous - an ebullient explorer of a world that seems new:

(she'd) **Rather leap from a height than anything...**
Jump straight out...into the summer morning

Even the darkness of life is faced down with bracing brio: It is the lanes that are 'scared' of men in cars and, having raised this spectre, the poem does not linger over it; enjambement ensures breezy onwards movement to another danger embraced with characteristic enthusiasm:

To lunge out over the water

All these images present the girl alone. The final image depicts her utterly absorbed in 'peeling a ripe scab', savouring the painful sensation and then the sensual experience of tasting it on her tongue. The image vividly captures her uninhibited fascination with experience, her complete, individual self-sufficiency, her freedom from social mores.

Her adult self

The poem is, of course, constructed around a central antithesis. The narrator

presents herself, self-deprecatingly, as the opposite to her youthful self. A writer's life can be rather sedentary. Whereas her young self is characterised by dynamic verbs, 'run', 'climb', 'leap', 'lunge' and so forth, the older self's verb express regretful feelings, not movement: 'I have spoiled', 'I'd like to say', 'I have fears', 'I leave you'. Even the verbs need ancillaries. The adult self is full of sorrow and remorse, seeking forgiveness for having 'spoiled' her body. Carefreeness is replaced by having to move 'careful of a bad back'; fearlessness by having 'fears enough for us both'. In fact, the speaker ruefully admits that her two selves 'have nothing in common'.

The unmetred, unrhymed prose-like form of the poem, coupled with its lack of figurative or showy poetic techniques - figurative language is noticeable by its absence - make it seem direct, unguarded and honest. Our attention is directed not to poetic pyrotechnics, but to the speaking voice and is concentrated on the poignant relationship. The subtle sense of building up and dying away in the stanza pattern leaves the reader with a haunting sense of loss.

Crunch Time

MUST – GONE – TIGHTROPE – CLIMB – ANYTHING – SPOILED – SCARS – CAREFUL – REMEMBER – JUMP – MORNING – DREAM – WHITE – START – VOLE – AMBITION – ICE-LOLLY – DEN – LIKE – TRUTH – SHARED – TUPPENCE – HIDE – MEN – LUNGE – ROPE – BURIED – CLOUD – FEARS – ECSTASY – RIPE – TONGUE.

With its Blakelan theme of innocence and experience and use of antithesis as a central structural element, *To My Nine-Year-Old Self* links to *A Leisure Centre is Also a Temple of Learning* and *An Easy Passage*. Its portrait of selfhood also links it to *Inheritance* and *Genetics*.

U. A. Fanthorpe: *a minor role*

In the centre of the picture above are the central characters from Sophocles' Greek Tragedy, **Oedipus the King**, the protagonist, Oedipus, and his mother and wife, Jocasta. If U. A. Fanthorpe were in this picture she'd probably be the silhouetted figure at the back left. Fanthorpe's poignant, stoical poem celebrates the quiet heroism of unglamorous, but essential secondary roles and the sort of people who modestly, unostentatiously, uncomplainingly perform them.

Think of a hero or heroine and what sort of images spring readily to mind? The world of Hollywood seems at present to be dominated by muscle-bound, super-powered, super heroes - beings who are stronger, faster, just, well all round better, than mere mortals. Fanthorpe's poem offers a different type of quiet, selfless heroism.

Like *Gallipoli, A Minor Role* is a list poem, busily full of ordinary, everyday verbs. Seemingly the poet herself, its protagonist is described as 'propping', 'making', 'driving', 'parking', 'holding', 'making sense of', 'asking', 'checking', 'getting on', and 'sustaining'. Repetition of all these present continuous tense verbs conveys the sense of endless and unending, mundane, but essential, chores. Syntax reinforces this impression. Look, for instance, at the last six lines of the second stanza: Each sentence fragment follows a very similar pattern. Notice too how the grammatically incomplete sentence, starting with 'Holding hands under/ veteran magazines' ending at 'civility', lacks one thing, a subject, the speaker who performs all these unherculean tasks. It's another way in which the poem's narrator slips easily into the background, even in her own poem.

Repetition occurs too across stanzas: Relocated from the hospital to the home, the second half of the third stanza follows a similar pattern to the previous stanza. Again we have a list of actions, the terms of which are again separated by neat semi-colons; again each item in the list starts with a verb, again in the present tense: 'answer'; 'contrive', 'find'. This sequence ends with a quickening flurry, as if the pressure is increasing: 'cancel', 'tidy', pretend', 'admit'. Of course, these last two verbs contradict each other; the impression of everything being under control is just that, an impression, an act. Underneath the appearance of coping, the narrator is, in reality, struggling to deal with a very traumatic situation. Even when a major break in the narrative is signalled by the use of three stars, the next stanza begins mid-sentence and immediately with another present continuous verb, one that evinces continual struggle, 'enduring'. All the while the poem's hard-pressed, industrious narrator is uncomplaining. Maintaining her composure and good manners, she asks questions 'politely', is 'grateful always', sustains 'the background music of civility', says 'thank you/ for anything to everyone'. Hence the reader is encouraged to feel sympathy and respect for this quiet form of domestic heroism.

ing together a number of features generate the poem's briskness:

- a preponderance of verbs
- truncated sentences
- the listing pattern
- repetitive syntax
- a pervasive use of enjambement.

It's as if the narrator relentlessly presses on in order to suppress any feelings of self-pity that might otherwise surface. And, as the poem's title and opening allusion to acting indicate, the narrator is also aware of the pressure to keep up appearances, to play their part well. In other words, the poem's breeziness embodies the stoical attitude the narrator strikes for society. In poetic form it is the analogue of the 'formula' the speaker adopts to ward off 'well-meant intrusiveness'.

That the situation really is difficult and traumatic becomes explicit in fourth stanza. Here the subtle linguistic metaphor of conjugation recalls all the previous verbs in the poem, all the stuff with which the narrator has had to cope. Conjugating 'all the genres of misery' suggests experiencing lots of suffering, 'tears, torpor' and so forth, but also a method for dealing with it. Working in combination with the literary metaphor of 'genres', the verb 'conjugate' implies a certain emotional distance on the experience, an ability to pull back and observe, or read it. To conjugate a verb implies understanding and control. Indeed, it may make us wonder, if we haven't already, whether the narrator is referring to her own misery or to someone else's.

The speaker in this poem is so self-effacing that it is not clear whether she is the ill party taking herself off to hospital and then caring for herself back at home. If she is speaking about her own illness, the distance between the busy narrative voice and the experiences depicted would signal the narrator's ability to step outside her own experience, observe and hence manage it. But perhaps, there is another silent, unnamed character in the poem, someone the speaker is actually looking after. In this second reading the 'hunger-striker' for whom the narrator is preparing meals is not herself, but her partner.

Which do you think would make a more convincing interpretation?
To me, the second of these two readings is more credible. The poem's speaker tells us that habitually she takes a secondary, ancillary role. With her 'servant's patter' she does not take what she calls the 'star part'; she maintains the 'background music'. In the poem's narrative the main protagonist, the starring part, is surely the ill person; most of the action

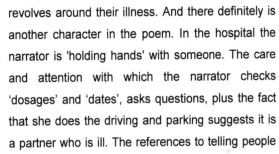

revolves around their illness. And there definitely is another character in the poem. In the hospital the narrator is 'holding hands' with someone. The care and attention with which the narrator checks 'dosages' and 'dates', asks questions, plus the fact that she does the driving and parking suggests it is a partner who is ill. The references to telling people things are 'getting better', making meals for a 'hunger striker' and wanting a 'simpler illness' could, perhaps, be read either way. It seems more probable, however, that the cook and the hunger-striker are, in fact, two different people; that the narrator as carer is trying to make her ill partner eat.

If we read the poem as being about the partner's illness, not the narrator's, the last line also becomes freighted with greater urgency and emotional resonance:

I am here to make you believe in life

The 'you' in this reading is made more intimate and personal. This pronoun refers to us, the readers, of course, but also to an ailing beloved, silently present, listening in. The two readings subtly affect the tone of the line too: Addressed just to the reader, the tone is declarative and defiant; addressed to a beloved the line takes on an undertone, becoming almost a plea. Again extra poignancy is added. So, while both readings are valid, I'm inclined to favour the idea that this Fanthorpe's poem is about a relationship. Whichever way we read the poem, in the end, though, it is the narrator's heroic stoicism that comes through most strongly.

Why does the poet use free verse?

Fanthorpe's poem does not rhyme, nor is there a regular metre. The stanzas are also irregular - the last one just one line long. And yet, on the page, the poem looks fairly orderly. Clearly there is a sense in which the poem's form enacts the narrator's experience: Difficult, destabilising, emotional experience is wrestled into some sort of control – into words and sentences and stanzas - but is not contained by a reliable, predictable external pattern, such as a set poetic form. We have already mentioned the preponderance of enjambement; caesurae are used as frequently. Many of the poem's sentences start in the middle of lines, run over line ends, becoming long, winding lists. It is as if the stable form of the poem has been knocked slightly awry; order here is under intense pressure from forces of disorder. Though lines run over each other, each stanza finishes with an emphatic full stop. Like the narrator, the form of the poem may be subject to intense external strain, but it is holding fast, holding on. Just about. Or so it appears from the outside.

A few times prominent spaces are left between lines:

1. **For well-meant intrusiveness.**

   At home,

2. **For anything to everyone**

   Not the star part.

What might this striking typography convey?

In the first example, a significant separation is implied between the other people and the narrator. A sense of isolation is emphasised by the words 'at home' being stuck at the end of the line, preceded by emptiness and silence. In the plays of Shakespeare and Harold Pinter, silences invite the audience to fill in a character's unspoken thoughts. In the second example, the implication of the first lines are left to linger for a while and, as with the first example, the most important words are emphasised by having a line to themselves, not at the prominent start however, but shunted to the back.

Expressed in an unshowy, 'unobtrusive', modest kind of language, Fanthorpe's poem is, as we have said, about a modest kind of heroism. But there's intellectual sophistication and steel underneath the self-effacing exterior. It takes courage to reject the wisdom handed down by great works of literature. Fanthorpe quotes from the chorus on *Oedipus Rex* only to reject its sentiment emphatically: 'No it wouldn't'. Though the poem is full of ordinary everyday chores, the poet makes clear that these activities are not futile or inconsequential. In a poem composed mostly of literal language, Fanthorpe employs metaphors to ensure that these moments stand out:

- the 'monstrous fabric' of a play depends on the 'midget moments' being performed correctly
- the poet's actions at the hospital sustain, 'the background music of civility'

A reader might conclude that the poem's title should, in fact, be read ironically. What more major role can anyone play than making us believe in life?

Crunch Time

STAGE – ENDLESS – SERVANT'S – SIR – MONSTROUS – SHRINKS – UNOBTRUSIVE – ROLES – HOLDING – SENSE – ASKING – CHECKING – DATES – BACKGROUND – HOME – FAST – FORMULA – INTRUSIVENESS – HOME – BED – SOLVES – WARY – HUNGER-STRIKER – HAPPY – REASSURING – PRETEND – ADMIT – MISERY –

TEARS – SIMPLER – ENDURING – THANK – EVERYONE – STAR – WANT – TERRIBLE – ILL-ADVISED – DIE – BELIEVE.

Dealing with coping with suffering and relationships (with the self or with a partner), concerned with identity, _**A Minor Role**_ could be linked to **Inheritance**, and **The Map-Woman**. The traumatic nature of the experiences depicted in the poem could link it too to **Effects** and **On her Blindness**.

Vicki Feaver: *the gun*

What thoughts spring to mind when you read the first couple of lines of this poem?

Bringing a gun into a house

Changes it.

A home is a place of safety. Imagine a gun brought into your own house. How would your family react? What possible reason could there be for its arrival? How would it change the atmosphere?

Immediately in these two lines the poet establishes a sense of tension and danger. Notice how the poet uses space to generate suspense:

• A mini-space is left between the first line and the second. Feaver could just as easily have written the sentence as one line, not two. Which option is more effective? Why?
• These two lines are isolated from the body of the poem - another brief space for us to contemplate the lines' significance

• The poet doesn't give too much away; we know the gun changes things, but she doesn't tell us how, another space for our speculation to fill

• A fourth uncertain semantic space is created by the non-specific pronoun 'it', which can refer to the gun or the house. For now, the resolution of meaning remains suspended.

We are then introduced to a second person, the poem's auditor, 'you' who has brought in the gun. Unhurried lines convey unhurried action. The poem's paradoxical theme is subtly suggested: The gun is itself 'like something dead'. In the last four lines of this stanza there is a tightening of syntax and attention: Shorter lines contain a series of concentrated still images, one per line. Ominous details signal the gun's potential danger: 'jutting over the edge', for example, implies transgression, the crossing boundaries. The phrase 'Over the edge' implies losing control. The poet increases the foreshadowing – a 'shadow', for instance, is a common poetic metaphor for a ghost.

The tone changes with the casual sounding, looser, more conversational, 'At first it's just practice'. But this stanza moves swiftly - suddenly from harmless shooting of inanimate objects to killing a rabbit by shooting it through the head. The level of violence escalates unnervingly fast. In this light, 'at first' becomes more ominous; if this is what happens 'at first' what might happen, we wonder, 'at last'? The word 'shadow' hovers in the poem's tense atmosphere.

Feaver's poem is in free verse. No metre or rhyme scheme determines either line or stanza length. Or, indeed, the overall length of the poem. This structural looseness means the lines in the poem are hard to predict – they are not following a predetermined pattern which the ear and the eye can anticipate. <u>What stops free verse poems being prose randomly arranged into something just looking like verse?</u>

Firstly the stanzas themselves; some principle must structure them. As we have already noted, in **The Gun**, for instance, there is clear design in the isolation of the first two lines. Subsequent stanzas outline the stages of a narrative. In the second, the gun is brought into the kitchen; in the third is put to use; the fourth stanza outlines the results of the gun's use; an isolated line follows, echoing, but modulating, the opening and the poem concludes with how the poet/ the poet's persona reacts. Secondly, lineation, the choice of where to start and end lines, is particularly important in free verse. A good rule of thumb is to assume the poet has put careful thought into this element of structure. Try re-arranging the lines, as we did with the opening two, to highlight the effects of the poet's choices. If the lineation is not purposeful then we do indeed have prose chopped up and dressing itself up as poetry. The middle lines from Feaver's fourth stanza illustrate her precise lineation:

Your hands reek of gun oil
And entrails.

Four elements of arrangement come together here to generate impact:
• the choice of syntax, so that the most important aspect comes at the end of the sentence
• a small delay, created by cutting the line before 'and entrails'
• the placing of this phrase at the start of the next line
• the caesura after 'and entrails', allowing its full effect to sink in. And linger.

Compare, for instance, an alternative arrangement:

Your hands reek of entrails and gun oil.

Here we have exactly the same words and broadly the same meaning, but all the tension, the shock impact of 'and entrails' has been lost.

The central theme of the poem, that closeness to death and killing paradoxically makes us feel more alive, is made more explicit at the end of the fourth stanza. The 'you' character is rejuvenated; they feel more alive, more youthful, more energetic: 'There's a spring/ in your step/ your eyes gleam/ like when sex was fresh'. The language of the poem is also invigorated here; sibilance, a stronger, more emphatic rhythm and running assonance combine to put a spring in the poem's quickening stride. In fact, the rhythm becomes almost a regular anapaestic one:

There's a **spring**
De de DUM

In your **step**, your eyes **gleam**
De de DUM, de de DUM

Like when **sex** was **fresh**
De de DUM de DUM

Here the close semantic connection between the words 'carnivore' and 'carnal' spring to mind. Resumption of the role of hunter has wakened other powerful, sensual appetites. After this quickening, there is a pause. And then Feaver delivers the long delayed information about exactly how the house has been changed:

A gun brings a house alive.

<u>What's surprising about this line?</u> Clearly as the gun is a bringer of death it's paradoxical that it can bring something back to life, like a miracle cure. Tonally too, the line's surprising. Up until this line the attitude of the poem's speaker to

the introduction of the gun has remained tensely uncertain. Now, it seems, despite the gruesome entrails and the heap of dead animals. the speaker is not appalled, as we might have suspected; rather they too are excited, caught up in the increased intensity that the gun has brought to the couple's life. To say the least, this is not a stereotypically female response to

violence, bloodshed and the piling up of carcasses.

The final stanza sees the speaker take their full part in the bloody enterprise. There is no squeamishness; like their partner, they are 'excited' as they perform a series of transformative actions which swiftly turn bloody carcass into meal. The poem ends with an extraordinary simile that relocates the action into some sort of mythical or fairy tale dimension. The figure of 'The King of Death' suggests both the Greek God Hades and the Grim Reaper, but is, I think, Feaver's own invention. The medieval, fairy tale flavour of 'King of Death' is enhanced by the reference to his arrival 'to feast' from the 'winter woods'. It is as if the awesome figure of the 'King of Death' has been released into their dimension by the couple's return to hunting their meat – a huntsman, of course, is a key character in fairy tales. Out of his ominously 'black mouth' are sprouting 'golden crocuses'. Here the central paradoxical idea of the poem - that more intense life comes from closeness to death - is made concrete in a brilliantly visual, evocative image. Out of death's mouth new flowers blossom; beautiful and precious flowers - they are 'golden'.

According to Oxford Journals online the crocus species 'in spring are a symbol of the awakening of nature, of resurrection, even of heavenly bliss'. Saffron is produced from crocuses and, in classical literature, is the colour of the robe worn by the dawn and by Hymen, god of weddings. Both these associations fit with the idea of a new bright beginning, emanating from death.

Crunch Time

The poem crunched:

HOUSE - CHANGES – KITCHEN – DEAD – WOOD – JUTTING – BARREL – SHADOW – GREEN – JUST – TINS – ORANGE – GARDEN – RABBIT – HEAD – CREATURES – RUN – REEK – ENTRAILS – SPRING – GLEAM – SEX – ALIVE – JOIN – SLICING – DEATH – FEAST – WOODS – BLACK – CROCUSES.

For **_The Gun_** the question could ask about male and female relationships or the concentration on the effect of one object. Good comparison poems include **A Leisure Centre is also a Temple of Learning**, **The Map-Woman** and **Eat Me**. **The Lammas Hireling** also explores the effect of a new element entering the domestic space.

Revision

Genuine poetry can communicate before it is understood.

T. S. Eliot

A sonnet of revision activities

1. Top ten poems. Each student ranks the poems in a top ten selection, writing brief reasons for their choices. One student writes their top ten on the whiteboard. Others are then invited to knock one poem out and to move one poem up or down. The aim is to arrive at class consensus

2. Top ten lines – ditto

3. Group the poems according to different aspects, form, theme, tone, language, context. Ideally use a big piece of paper and colouring pens and make as many links as possible

4. Use Venn diagrams to visualise shared details between poems

5. Visualise a poem: Present it as a single picture or diagram that captures its essence

6. Turn it into a storyboard for a film. Think of the transitions between stanzas as different film shots; are they cross-cuts, fades, dissolves? What sort of soundtrack does the film need? What are the ambient sounds? For a brilliant example of a film poem check out *The Black Delph Bride* by Liz Berry: ttps://www.youtube.com/watch?v=JT0izGJCHO8

7. Match the poem with another text. This can be an image, a song, a memory, an extract from a Geography text book, but it has to be something that makes the poem resonate in a new light

8. If the poem were a piece of music what would it be? Which poems are the poetic equivalent of death metal, free form jazz or gangsta rap, which are more like your favourite classical piece?

9. Apply critical theories to the poems. What would a Feminist critic make

of Armitage's poem? Why might a Marxist be interested in *Eat Me*? Turn the concise descriptions on different theories in *The Art of Writing English Literature Essays, for A-level and Beyond*, into cards, put a class in pairs with one poem each. They have five minutes to try to apply each card to the poem. Alternatively, all the class examine the same poem but each pair is given a different critical perspective. Discuss findings

10. Write questions to ask each poet about their poem. Swap with another student and try to answer the questions they have written

11. Place the poems on a continuum with radically experimental at one pole and well-made/ conventional/ traditional at the other. Try this task taking the poem as a whole and then try it again, breaking the poems down to their constituent elements of form, language, topic. Some poems, for instance, might be radical in terms of topic but conventional in terms of form. Agbabi's *Eat Me*, for instance, might fall into this category

12. Write sample paragraphs on key aspects of each poem. A paragraph just on figurative imagery, another on the poet's use of sonic devices

13. Write a response to the poem in any form you like. You are the mother in *Material*, the daughters in *Inheritance*, Lukas in *History*. Write your thoughts in whatever form you like

14. Play a variation of the popular Radio 4 panel game, *The Unbelievable Truth*. Each student has to write a two minute speech about a poem from the Anthology. During their speech they have to try to smuggle 5 lies about the poem past the rest of the class. The rest of the class have to try to spot these lies.

Critical soundbites

In this demanding revision activity, students have to match the following excerpts from criticism to the poet whose work they describe. (Answers are at the end of this book):

1. Her poems deal with private and communal loss, a theme established by the opening poem...the poet combines elegiac thoughts...with touching memories.

2. The poet's perennial themes are love and loss, the transience of nature and of human lives.

3. The poet weaves different and competing kinds of history—the national, the personal, the domestic—together in poems that also meditate on the legacy of Irish poetry itself.

4. Their poems try to disentangle past, present and future, yet court situations in which such divisions are blurred.

5. Their poems move from domesticity into the territory of folk tales, Biblical stories, Greek myths, paintings and dreams. Her work is emotional but cunning, and like proverbial Nature, at times red in tooth and claw.

6. Formally elegant, lightly constructed, her poems provocatively explore the sadness and happiness of life – from ancient Rome, Renaissance Italy, revolutionary Paris, to today, we see courage in the face of love and loss, wry humour and acceptance when confronted with sorrow.

7. Dark shadows, childhood traumas, the close presences of the dead, and above all the omnipresence of death throughout life; all these elements recur throughout his poetry

8. Their poems possess a vitality...a heightened chattiness that combines idiomatic cliché with arresting and often unusual observations and descriptions, spanning his favoured territory of tall tales, humorous dramatic monologues and often sinister, noirish anecdotes.

9. Their poetry revels in exploring the complex flux of the world as we variously experience it: bringing an exacting eye, taut rhythms and often vivid language to our subjectively skewed perspectives.

10. The poet's distinctive use of the long line...frees the poet to plunge further into the chaotic webs created by the intersections of language, history and geography.

11. The poet's themes include language and the representation of reality; the construction of the self; gender issues; contemporary culture; and many different forms of alienation, oppression and social inequality.

12. A formalist, often adapting traditional forms such as sonnets and sestinas to (the poet's) own gender-bending sexual politics.

13. Their poems are intellectually challenging, at times arcane, though often written in populist forms such as ballads, folksongs or rhyming quatrains.

14. Exploring issues of identity in taut, lyrical style, the poet combines an acute ear for the music of life with a painterly eye for its most revealing details.

Poetry is finer and more philosophical than history; for poetry expresses the universal, and history only the particular.

Aristotle

Glossary

ALLITERATION – the repetition of consonants at the start of neighbouring words in a line

ANAPAEST - a three beat pattern of syllables, unstress, unstress, stress. E.g. 'on the moon', 'to the coast', 'anapaest'

ANTITHESIS - the use of balanced opposites

APOSTROPHE – a figure of speech addressing a person, object or idea

ASSONANCE – vowel rhyme, e.g. sod and block

BLANK VERSE – unrhymed lines of iambic pentameter

BLAZON – a male lover describing the parts of his beloved

CADENCE – the rise of fall of sounds in a line of poetry

CAESURA – a distinct break in a poetic line, usually marked by punctuation

COMPLAINT – a type of love poem concerned with loss and mourning

CONCEIT – an extended metaphor

CONSONANCE – rhyme based on consonants only, e.g. book and back

COUPLET – a two line stanza, conventionally rhyming

DACTYL – the reverse pattern to the anapaest; stress, unstress, unstress. E.g. 'Strong as a'

DRAMATIC MONOLOGUE – a poem written in the voice of a distinct character

ELEGY – a poem in mourning for someone dead

END-RHYME – rhyming words at the end of a line

END-STOPPED – the opposite of enjambment; i.e. when the sentence and the poetic line stop at the same point

ENJAMBMENT – where sentences run over the end of lines and stanzas

FIGURATIVE LANGUAGE – language that is not literal, but employs figures of speech, such as metaphor, simile and personification

FEMININE RHYME – a rhyme that ends with an unstressed syllable or unstressed syllables.

FREE VERSE – poetry without metre or a regular, set form

GOTHIC – a style of literature characterised by psychological horror, dark deeds and uncanny events

HEROIC COUPLETS – pairs of rhymed lines in iambic pentameter

HYBERBOLE – extreme exaggeration

IAMBIC – a metrical pattern of a weak followed by a strong stress, ti-TUM, like a heart beat

IMAGERY – the umbrella term for description in poetry. Sensory imagery refers to descriptions that appeal to sight, sound and so forth; figurative imagery refers to the use of devices such as metaphor, simile and personification

JUXTAPOSITION – two things placed together to create a strong contrast

LYRIC – an emotional, personal poem usually with a first person speaker

MASCULINE RHYME – an end rhyme on a strong syllable

METAPHOR – an implicit comparison in which one thing is said to be another

METAPHYSICAL – a type of poetry characterised by wit and extended metaphors

METRE – the regular pattern organising sound and rhythm in a poem

MOTIF – a repeated image or pattern of language, often carrying thematic significance

OCTET OR OCTAVE – the opening eight lines of a sonnet

ONOMATOPOEIA – bang, crash, wallop

PENTAMETER – a poetic line consisting of five beats

PERSONIFICATION – giving human characteristics to inanimate things

PLOSIVE – a type of alliteration using 'p' and 'b' sounds

QUATRAIN – a four line stanza

REFRAIN – a line or lines repeated like a chorus

ROMANTIC – A type of poetry characterised by a love of nature, by strong emotion and heightened tone

SESTET – the last six lines in a sonnet

SIMILE – an explicit comparison of two different things

SONNET – a form of poetry with fourteen lines and a variety of possible set rhyme patterns

SPONDEE – two strong stresses together in a line of poetry

STANZA – the technical name for a verse

SYMBOL – something that stands in for something else. Often a concrete representation of an idea.

SYNTAX – the word order in a sentence. doesn't Without sense English syntax make.

TERCET – a three line stanza

TETRAMETER – a line of poetry consisting of four beats

TROCHEE – the opposite of an iamb; stress, unstress, strong, weak.

VILLANELLE – a complex interlocking verse form in which lines are recycled

VOLTA – the 'turn' in a sonnet from the octave to the sestet

Recommended reading

For the committed reader there's a brilliant overview of developments in English poetry in Part 2 of *The Oxford English Literary History, volume 12,* by Randall Stevenson.

More general books on writing, reading & analysing poetry:

Atherton, C. & Green, A. *Teaching English Literature 16-19*. NATE, 2013

Bowen et al. *The Art of Poetry, vol.1*. Peripeteia Press, 2015

Brinton, I. *Contemporary Poetry*. CUP, 2009

Eagleton, T. *How to Read a Poem*. Wiley & Sons, 2006

Fry, S. *The Ode Less Travelled*. Arrow, 2007

Heaney, S. *The Government of the Tongue*. Farrar, Straus & Giroux, 1976

Herbert, W. & Hollis, M. *Strong Words*. Bloodaxe, 2000

Meally, M. & Bowen, N. *The Art of Writing English Literature Essays,* Peripeteia Press, 2014

Maxwell, G. *On Poetry*. Oberon Masters, 2012

Padel, R. *52 Ways of Looking at a Poem*. Vintage, 2004

Padel, R. *The Poem and the Journey*. Vintage, 2008

Paulin, T. *The Secret Life of Poems*. Faber & Faber, 2011

Wolosky, S. *The Art of Poetry: How to Read a Poem*. OUP, 2008.

About the author

An experienced Head of English and freelance writer, **Neil Bowen** is the author of many articles and resources for a range of publishers. Neil has a Masters Degree in Literature and Education from Cambridge University and he is a member of Ofqual's experts panel for English. He is the author of *The Art of Writing English Essays for GCSE* and co-author of *The Art of Writing English Essays for A-level and beyond* and *The Art of Poetry, volume 1*. Neil has also recently edited *Angleland*, a book on Anglo-Saxon history, and runs the peripeteia project: www.perirpeteia.webs.com

With thanks to **Matthew Curry** for his invaluable help, support and advice.

Answers to critical soundbites:

1. Barber
2. Dunmore
3. Boland
4. Doshi
5. Feaver
6. Boyle
7. Burnside
8. Armitage
9. Copus
10. Carson
11. Duffy
12. Agbabi
13. Duhig
14. None of the above; made-up by the author. There's no soundbite for Fanthorpe: A final revision task might be to find a good one.

Critical soundbites adapted from:
https://literature.britishcouncil.org

http://www.toppingbooks.co.uk

http://www.poetryfoundation.org

http://www.theguardian.com

Printed in Great Britain
by Amazon